JESUS DEORTHODOXED

ESCAPING THE CORRUPTION IN THE WORLD

STEPHEN CLOPTON

WESTBOW
PRESS®
A DIVISION OF THOMAS NELSON
& ZONDERVAN

WestBow Press books may be ordered through booksellers or by contacting:

WestBow Press
A Division of Thomas Nelson & Zondervan
1663 Liberty Drive
Bloomington, IN 47403
www.westbowpress.com
844-714-3454

All scripture quotations are taken from the King James Version. Public domain.

ISBN: 978-1-9736-9882-1 (sc)
ISBN: 978-1-9736-9881-4 (e)

Library of Congress Control Number: 2023910216

Print information available on the last page.

WestBow Press rev. date: 06/09/2023

INTRODUCTION

As I brush away some wax from the table top and close the window because the sound of horsemen is distracting, I ask myself what is behind the "Bride of Christ" allegory? Yes, it helps us have more of an understanding of His love and compassion towards us, but is there something we have missed in this common correlation? If we go back to Genesis to the creation of man we can see that he, man, was created in the image of God and man was created both male and female.

26 And God said, Let us make man in our image, after our likeness: and let them have dominion over the fish of the sea, and over the fowl of the air, and over the cattle, and over all the earth, and over every creeping thing that creepeth upon

27 So God created man in his own image, in the image of God created he him; male and female created he them - Genesis 1:26-27

I have always been led to believe that in was a cinematic experience where everything spoken by God took on form as the words left his mouth but if you read the story and not just read into it what you have been taught you start to see something different

"And the Lord God formed man from the dust of the ground, and breathed into his nostrils the breath of life; and man became a living soul." – Genesis 2:7

So at this point we have man and 2 stories of the creation of man. Genesis 2:5 helps separate the events of Genesis 1 and 2.

....there was not a man to till the ground. – Genesis 2:5

And the Lord God formed man of the dust of the ground, and breathed into his nostrils the breath of life; and man became a living soul. (Genesis 2:7)

Man, like everything else has to be created before it can be formed

Then in the garden, out of the ground, made the Lord God to grow every tree that is pleasant to the sight, and good for food.

-Genesis 2:9

This is a paradigm shift because I have always taught that God spoke it and it appeared. Hebrews provides more of an explanation.

"Through faith we understand that the worlds were framed by the word of God, so that things which are seen were not made of things which do appear." – Hebrews 11:3

So all of the things in Genesis 1 were spoken and created in faith: the power of the invisible, and then God created them from the dust of the ground (Genesis 2:7, 9,19).

"For the invisible things of him from the creation of the world are clearly seen, being understood by the things that are made, even his eternal power and Godhead; so that they are without excuse." – Romans 1:20

And then...

"the Lord God said, It is not good that the man should be alone; I will make him an help meet for him. And "out of the ground" the Lord God formed every beast of the field, and every fowl of the air; and brought them unto Adam to see what he would call them: and whatsoever Adam called every living creature, that was the name there of and Adam gave names to all cattle, and to the fowl of the air, and to every beast of the field; but for Adam there was not found an help meet for him." - Genesis 2:18-20

So, we then have Adam naming all of the cattle and fowl and beast but there was not found a help meet. Now this is interesting because it seems provide an answer to the dinosaur question, not directly, but if you believe man is an image of God then it would be safe to assume that everything we experience God experienced on some level. The leap I am trying to make is, God: both male and female, wanted a help meet also and He created dinosaurs: beast of the field, and every fowl of the air.

Psalms 104

28 That thou givest them they gather: thou openest thine hand, they are filled with good.

29 Thou hidest thy face, they are troubled: thou takest away their breath, they die, and return to their dust.

30 Thou sendest forth thy spirit, they are created: and thou renewest the face of the earth.

This I believe is a reference to the creation and extinction of dinosaurs: a beast of the field you might say. He wasn't satisfied with dinosaurs and returned them to dust which is where fossils come from. He renewed the face of the earth and decided to make Man in his own image. He formed from the earth an earthen vessel and breathed part of himself into it: the Spirit. We see the same type of thing happen (taking out of one to form two) with man…

"21 And the Lord God caused a deep sleep to fall upon Adam, and he slept: and he took one of his ribs, and closed up the flesh instead thereof; 22 And the rib, which the Lord God had taken from man, made he a woman, and brought her unto the man." – Genesis 2: 21-22

Rib in verse 22 is Strong's H6763 and means: side, rib, beam, can also be used to describe "side-chambers or cells (of temple structure)".

This is interesting because 1 Corinthians 6:19 says that out bodies are temples of God.

This is why we, believers, are referred to as a "bride" in the Bible because man, when filled with the spirit, has the female part of God. The Holy Spirit is referred to as the comforter: g3875 – summoned, called to one's side, esp. called to one's aid. A "help meet" of sorts. The same thing He said man needed.

This presentation of truth is a way that the natural reflects the spiritual (Romans 1:20)

Sin is anoun

"1 Now the serpent was more subtle than any beast of the field which the Lord God had made. And he said unto the woman, Yea, hath God said, Ye shall not eat of every tree of the garden? 2 And the woman said unto the serpent, We may eat of the fruit of the trees of the garden: 3 But of the fruit of the tree which is in the midst of the garden, God hath said, Ye shall not eat of it, neither shall ye touch it, lest ye die. 4 And the serpent said unto the woman, Ye shall not surely die: 5 For God doth know that in the day ye eat thereof, then your eyes shall be opened, and ye shall be as gods, knowing good and evil." – Genesis 3:1-5

I read this and think to myself, serpents talked? I believe I have located the answer to the question.

"6 And the Lord sent fiery serpents among the people, and they bit the people; and much people of Israel died. 7 Therefore the people came to Moses, and said, We have sinned, for we have spoken against the Lord, and against thee; pray unto the Lord, that he take away the serpents from us. And Moses prayed for the people. 8 And the Lord said unto Moses, Make thee a fiery serpent, and set it upon a pole: and it shall come to pass, that every one that is bitten, when he looketh upon it, shall live. 9 And Moses made a serpent of brass, and put it upon a pole, and it came to pass, that if a serpent had bitten any man, when he beheld the serpent of brass, he lived." Number 21:5-9

I have always understood this to mean that God summoned poisonous snakes and they bit the people and the ones who did not gaze upon the serpent of brass died because fiery means poisonous

Fiery: H8314 – poisonous serpent.

The other meaning for the word translated as fiery is majestic beings with 6 wings, human hands or voices in attendance upon God. This is the same word translated as Seraphim in Isaiah 6:2,6.

Going back to Genesis 3, when Eve had an interaction with the (seraphim) serpent, she was quick to answer with what God had said (Genesis 3:4) but God never said that to Eve specifically, God said this to Adam when he was still male and female.

"16 And the Lord God commanded the man, saying, Of every tree of the garden thou mayest freely eat: 17 But of the tree of the knowledge of good and evil, thou shalt not eat of it: for in the day that thou eatest thereof thou shalt surely die." – Genesis 2:16-17

The serpents, who I believe is sin, response to Eve gives us a little insight to what the temptation was: restoration. The serpent said "Ye shall be as gods". Eve was already a god created in the image of God but she was no longer defined as man or gods: both male and female. A person would have to go to the new testament to get a better understanding of what happened.

"Wherefore, as by one man (Adam and Eve) sin entered into the world, and death by sin; and so death passed upon all men, for that all have sinned." – Romans 5:12

What I see here is through one man's offence (Romans 5:17) sin entered the world; not one man's sin because sin was not in the world yet.

"Know ye not, that to whom ye yield yourselves servants to obey, his servants ye are to whom ye obey; whether of sin unto death, or of obedience unto righteousness?" – Romans 6:16

This tells me how death entered the world: Adam and Eve yielded themselves as servants to the serpent, or sin, and then death entered the world.

Romans 6:16 says if I served sin: who I believe is the serpent, death would enter the world. To me this conclusively makes sin and the serpent the same thing.

This goes deeper…

"And the great dragon was cast out, that old serpent, called the Devil, and Satan, which deceiveth the whole world: he was cast out into the earth, and his angels were cast out with him." - Revelation 12:9

Here we see the Devil being referred to as the serpent and this isn't my idea or conclusion because the Bible tells us so.

If you follow the structure of this sentence you can see that, first, the devil and satan are not the same because they are joined together by a conjunction. The job of a conjunction is, as the School House Rock song goes, "Hooking up words and phrases and clauses". This would mean that the devil and satan are not the same thing. Lets break this sentence down a little farther, we have the serpent who is the devil (emphasis added) and satan which deceived the whole world. Then we have a colon: which adds further explanation to what was previously said, The word "he" after the colon would be in reference to satan who was cast into the earth

The next part of this Is where I think some confusion comes in, "and his angels were cast out with him." This word translated into angels was translated as messenger in Paul's reference to the thorn in his flesh. This is where we can confirm that the devil is in the flesh and is sin using some other verses I will reference. So, put a pin in this

I believe everybody automatically thinks, "Oh, demons!" When they read angels because demons are supposedly fallen angels. This misunderstanding is perpetuated further by what I believe is the misunderstanding of a couple of other scriptures.

"How art thou fallen from heaven, O Lucifer, son of the morning! How art thou cut down to the ground, which didst weaken the nations!" – Isaiah 14:12

The understanding I once had of this is that Lucifer was referred to as a star so any reference to stars would be referring to Lucifer or his fallen angels.

Revelations 12:3-4

3 And there appeared another wonder in heaven; and behold a great red dragon, having seven heads and ten horns, and seven crowns upon his heads.

4 And his tail drew the third part of the stars of heaven, and did cast them to the earth: and the dragon stood before the woman which was ready to be delivered, for to devour her child as soon as it was born.

So it is easy to see why people assume that Lucifer drew a third of the angels with him to create his demons. With Lucifer, who is an angle, being referred to as a star and the ⅓ of the stars of God being drawn by the dragon's tail. Deductively, one can reach the conclusion that stars is a reference to other angels that fell to make demons.

But wait, there is more... Jesus is also referred to as a morning star..

"I, Jesus, have sent mine angel to testify unto you these things in the churches. I am the root and the offspring of David, and the bright and morning star." – Revelation 22:16

Lucifer's reference to "morning star" in Isaiah 14:12 was speaking to his brightness while Jesus' reference to the morning star was one of stature: the first of many. When we understand that Jesus is actually the morning star, it makes more sense why God told Abraham He, God, would make his descendants like stars (Genesis 15:5, 22:17, 26:4): God is going to adopt more sons or suns.

The fall

"For thou hast said in thine heart, I will ascend into heaven, I will exalt my throne above the stars of God: I will sit also upon the mount of the congregation, in the sides of the north." – Isaiah 14:13

Lucifer never said he would exalt himself above God: contrary to popular belief, but he did say he would exalt his throne above the stars of God: this would be Adam and Eve.

For thou hast made him a little lower than the angels, and hast crowned him with glory and honour. – Psalms 8:5

"I have said, Ye are gods; and all of you are children of the most High." – Psalm 82:6

I believe these to be words of knowledge inspired by the Lord through King David about man. These verses show that man is god: little g not a big G. Psalms 8:5 was transitory show man being a literal lower than angels but the word translated as angels is Strong's H430. H430 is the word elohim and speaks to God in the plural form which is a reference to the Trinity.

We now find ourselves in the garden, Lucifer was the anointed cherub that covereth and was in the garden to serve man: there was no difference between spiritual and physical before the fall and Lucifer walked around in the garden

Ezekiel 28:13-14

13 Thou hast been in Eden the garden of God; every precious stone was thy covering, the sardius, topaz, and the diamond, the beryl, the onyx, and the jasper, the sapphire, the emerald, and the carbuncle, and gold: the workmanship of thy tabrets and of thy pipes was prepared in thee in the day that thou wast created.

14 Thou art the anointed cherub that covereth; and I have set thee so: thou wast upon the holy mountain of God; thou hast walked up and down in the midst of the stones of fire.

We see that Lucifer was not a (Seraphim) serpent but was in the garden and was the anointed cherub the covereth. In the hierarchy of angels, we can understand through scripture, the Seraphim was lower than a Cherub and was subject to his, a Cherub's, authority. Lucifer sent an angel under his authority, or throne, a seraphim, to Eve and we have the story in Genesis 3: 1- 8 where Adam and Eve eat of the forbidden fruit.

"And the Lord God said unto the serpent, Because thou hast done this, thou art cursed above all cattle, and above every beast of the field; upon thy belly shalt thou go, and dust shalt thou eat all the days of thy life:" – Genesis 3:14

This is the point where sin came into the world.

"Wherefore, as by one man sin entered into the world..." – Romans 5:12

Now he, sin, was already in this world as a spiritual being on the side of light, but was cast into the physical world into the dust: darkness.

This is why 1 John 4:4 says "...he that is in the world." This is not Satan because the prince of the world, who was Satan, has been cast out according to John 12:31. Our bodies were formed by God from the dust of the world and by default would have sin in them: This is what Romans 7 is all about.

Now then it is no more I that do it, but sin that dwelleth in me. – Romans 7:17

The first sin

In Genesis 4, Cain and Abel were born. They both brought offerings to God. Able was the keeper of the sheep and offered to God the firstlings of his flock. Cain was a tiller of the ground and brought fruit from the ground. Now the Lord respects Abel's offering, but not Cain's because Abel's was the firstling, or the tithe, of his flock and the Bible says that Cain, "brought of the fruit of the ground an offering unto the Lord."

Genesis 4:6-7

6 And the Lord said unto Cain, Why art thou wroth? And why is thy countenance fallen?

7 If thou doest well, shalt thou not be accepted? And if thou doest not well, sin lieth at the door. And unto thee shall be his desire, and thou shalt rule over him.

What scripture is saying, from what I understand, if one did their best, why are they worried? If one didn't do their best, sin, or your flesh, has control over a person, but you need to rule over sin. Cain didn't take heed to Gods word and murdered Able. If we go to the new testament we can see that murder is a work of the flesh and the flesh is where sin is located.

Galatians 5

19 Now the works of the flesh are manifest, which are these; Adultery, fornication, uncleanness, lasciviousness,

20 Idolatry, witchcraft, hatred, variance, emulations, wrath, strife, seditions, heresies,

21 Envyings, murders, drunkenness, revellings, and such like: of the which I tell you before, as I have also told you in time past, that they which do such things shall not inherit the kingdom of God.

Going back to Revelations...

"And the great dragon was cast out, that old serpent, called the Devil, and Satan, which deceiveth the whole world: he was cast out into the earth, and his angels were cast out with him." - Revelation 12:9

I have already established the angels are not stars. Angels in Revelation 12:9 is in reference to the devil when

You follow the structure of the sentence. The word translated as angel is Strong's number G32, and was translated as angle 179 other times and messenger 7 other times. Where this really gets interesting is the same word translated as angels, in reference to the devil, is used in 2 Corinthians 12:7 as messenger

"And lest I should be exalted above measure through the abundance of the revelations, there was given to me a thorn in the flesh messenger of Satan to buffet me, lest I should be exalted above measure." – 2 Corinthians 12:7

"For this thing I besought the Lord thrice, that it might depart from me." – 2 Corinthians 12:8

God's answer brings more clarity (usually does).

"And he said unto me, My grace is sufficient for thee…" – 2 Corinthians 12:9

Where do we see grace?

"Moreover the law entered, that the offense might abound. But where sin abounded, grace did much more abound" – Romans 5:20

Where sin abounds…

"This is why we all need the grace of God to live because we all have a man of sin: the devil, in our flesh, or temples of God."

"For the flesh lusteth against the Spirit, and the Spirit against the flesh: and these are contrary one to the other: so that ye cannot do the things that ye would." – Galatians 5:17

So I think I have presented a good case as to who or what sin is and what happened in the garden and now a falling away is to come because of the revelation of the man of sin. I perceive that some might shake their head in disagreement saying, how can we know this? My response is Jesus. Jesus lives inside (2 Corinthians 13:5) and is the wisdom of God (1 Corinthians

1:24) and the wisdom of God is knowledge and understanding (Proverbs 2:6, Proverbs 9:10): to say you don't know or understand something is really a denial of Christ. The attitude of knowing is being spiritually minded while being carnally, or flesh, minded (Romans 8:6) keeps you attempting to be what you already are.

Book Start

We read the Old Testament and see God bless Abraham and make him prosper. This wasn't because he followed the law but because he believed: this was his saving work. God had told him that he would bear a seed

Galatians 3

14 That the blessing of Abraham might come on the Gentiles through Jesus Christ; that we might receive the promise of the Spirit through faith.

15 Brethren, I speak after the manner of men; Though it be but a man's covenant, yet if it be confirmed, no man disannulleth, or addeth thereto.

16 Now to Abraham and his seed were the promises made. He saith not, And to seeds, as of many; but as of one, And to thy seed, which is Christ.

17 And this I say, that the covenant, that was confirmed before of God in Christ, the law, which was four hundred and thirty years after, cannot disannul, that it should make the promise of none effect.

18 For if the inheritance be of the law, it is no more of promise: but God gave it to Abraham by promise.

This is the blessing God promised Abraham, he believed God and it was counted to him as righteousness: a promise fulfilled. He was the first of many that would be made righteous through believing. This was promised before there was a law, and is still the way we become righteous. It is made evident when we perform righteous acts. We work from a promise that God made Abraham, and not from a list of rules that were written in stone

Abraham was the beginning of the Nation of Israel and we can follow the lineage all the way to Joseph

https://en.wikipedia.org/wiki/Abraham%27s_family_tree

Joseph is who brought the Nation of Israel into Egypt but after a few generations Joseph was forgotten and the Israelites numbered in the millions. The Egyptians were scared and put them into slavery

Exodus

1 Now these are the names of the children of Israel, which came into Egypt; every man and his household came with Jacob.

2 Reuben, Simeon, Levi, and Judah,

3 Issachar, Zebulun, and Benjamin,

4 Dan, and Naphtali, Gad, and Asher.

5 And all the souls that came out of the loins of Jacob were seventy souls: for Joseph was in Egypt already.

6 And Joseph died, and all his brethren, and all that generation.

7 And the children of Israel were fruitful, and increased abundantly, and multiplied, and waxed exceeding mighty; and the land was filled with them.

8 Now there arose up a new king over Egypt, which knew not Joseph.

9 And he said unto his people, Behold, the people of the children of Israel are more and mightier than we:

10 Come on, let us deal wisely with them; lest they multiply, and it come to pass, that, when there falleth out any war, they join also unto our enemies, and fight against us, and so get them up out of the land.

11 Therefore they did set over them taskmasters to afflict them with their burdens. And they built for Pharaoh treasure cities, Pithom and Raamses.

There were about 2.4 million Israelites and they were there for about 430 years

https://www.gotquestions.org/Israelites-exodus.html

God raises up Moses as a leader through some various circumstances that were difficult but destiny is never an easy road. Moses was raised by his mother as a baby so I can assume he learned about his heritage that was. We don't know when that relationship stopped, but we do know that Moses was raised as royalty. He had the best food, schooling, training available at that time

And Moses was learned in all the wisdom of the Egyptians, and was mighty in words and deeds.
-Acts 7:22

We don't know how much of his lineage he understood, but when he saw one of his Hebrew brethren being mistreated he killed the abuser after making sure no one was looking

Exodus 2

11 And it came to pass in those days, when Moses was grown, that he went out unto his brethren, and looked on their burdens: and he spied an Egyptian smiting an Hebrew, one of his brethren.

12 And he looked this way and that way, and when he saw that there was no man, he slew the Egyptian, and hid him in the sand.

Moses feared for his life and ran to the dessert and dwelt in the land of Midian where he ran into a burning bush. Turns out it was God, and God told Moses he, Moses, was going to deliver the Israelites from Egypt. Some years pass and Moses Goes to Egypt to free the Israelites, and after some convincing, Pharaoh lets the Israelites leave. Pharaoh does a double take and realizes what he did and sent his army to go and catch them. Moses then parts the Red Sea and washes away the Egyptians, like sin, and the Israelites now have a new life where they are no longer slaves to sin..... I mean Egypt. They wander in the desert for 40 years trying to complete a journey that should have taken 11 days. Through all of their trial and tribulations they meet Jesus: as bread (manna) and (living) water (Jesus) from a rock (who also is Jesus). This helped sustain them on their journey.

And it came to pass on the morrow, that Moses sat to judge the people: and the people stood by Moses from the morning unto the evening.
Exodus 1813

Moses Father in law saw this wasn't good

And Moses' father in law said unto him, The thing that thou doest is not good.
Exodus 18:17

Jethro tells Moses to teach them to rule over themselves

And thou shalt teach them ordinances and laws, and shalt shew them the way wherein they must walk, and the work that they must do.
Exodus 18:20

Moses goes up to Mount Saini and comes back with the law and the Israelites said they could do what had been asked of them

And all the people answered together, and said, All that the Lord hath spoken we will do. And Moses returned the words of the people unto the Lord.
Exodus 19:8

Boom, there it is… The nation of Israel put themselves under the law because they said they could keep it. There was not another people groups there. God had made them a peculiar people

Now therefore, if ye will obey my voice indeed, and keep my covenant, then ye shall be a peculiar treasure unto me above all people: for all the earth is mine:
Exodus 19:5

The Covenant of the law of Moses was only made with one group of people: Israelites, and there was not another group of people that are Gods based on the Law of Moses The Israelites already partook of the blessing of Abraham because they were his decedents but Gentiles, who were not Israelites, had to be brought into the family

Galatians 3

14 That the blessing of Abraham might come on the Gentiles through Jesus Christ; that we might receive the promise of the Spirit through faith.

Fast Forward to Jesus….

A man, not from the seed of Adam, was born so that he could fulfill the law by being the last sacrifice for every group World.

For the life of the flesh is in the blood: and I have given it to you upon the altar to make an atonement for your souls: for it is the blood that maketh an atonement for the soul. – Leviticus 17:11
All of sins works sin have been atoned and Satan can no longer accuse an Israelite of not keeping the law and has never been able to accuse a Gentile for not keeping it

Then Peter had a vision

Acts 10

11 And saw heaven opened, and a certain vessel descending upon him, as it had been a great sheet knit at the four corners, and let down to the earth:

12 Wherein were all manner of fourfooted beasts of the earth, and wild beasts, and creeping things, and fowls of the air.

13 And there came a voice to him, Rise, Peter; kill, and eat.

14 But Peter said, Not so, Lord; for I have never eaten anything that is common or unclean.

15 And the voice spake unto him again the second time, What God hath cleansed, that call not thou common.

16 This was done thrice: and the vessel was received up again into heaven.

This is after Jesus Death and resurrection and The spirit of God was on the earth because sin no longer had dominion.

Nothing is unclean

And he said unto them, Ye know how that it is an unlawful thing for a man that is a Jew to keep company, or come unto one of another nation; but God hath shewed me that I should not call any man common or unclean – Acts 10:28

You can either accept that Jesus fulfilled the law that atones all sin or you can believe that we still live by the law and by that same law, not being an Israelite, you can consider yourself unclean.

This is what the bible has to say about a righteous man, which you are if you confess to be a disciple of Christ

1 Timothy 1

9knowing this, that the law is not made for a righteous man, but for the lawless and disobedient, for the ungodly and for sinners, for unholy and profane, for murderers of fathers and murderers of mothers, for manslayers, 10for whoremongers, for them that defile themselves with mankind, for menstealers, for liars, for perjured persons, and if there be any other thing that is contrary to sound doctrine; 11according to the glorious gospel of the blessed God, which was committed to my trust

You are not confessing your righteousness if you confess the law but there is a list of other actions the the Law is made for. I don't believe those are righteous?

Christ is become of no effect unto you, whosoever of you are justified by the law; ye are fallen from grace. – Galatians 5:4

The word translated as justified, G1344, means according to outline of biblical usage

To render righteous or such he ought to be
To show, exhibit, evince, one to be righteous, such as he is and wishes himself to be considered
To declare, pronounce, one to be just, righteous, or such as he ought to be

Strong's defines it as to render (i.e. show or regard as) just or innocent:— free, justify(-ier), be righteous.

If you are trying to get your righteousness from the law, which was never intended for a Gentile, then you are falling from grace and if you are saved by grace and you fall, are you still saved?

"For by grace are ye saved through faith; and that not of yourselves: [it is] the gift of God:" Ephesians 2:8

This is what Jesus has to say to trees (men and women) only covered in leaves (law) that don't grow any fruit (of the spirit)

Matthew 7:21-23

21 Not every one that saith unto me, Lord, Lord, shall enter into the kingdom of heaven; but he that doeth the will of my Father which is in heaven.

22 Many will say to me in that day, Lord, Lord, have we not prophesied in thy name? and in thy name have cast out devils? And in thy name done many wonderful works?

23 And then will I profess unto them, I never knew you: depart from me, ye that work iniquity.

Acts 10

35 But in every nation he that feareth him, and worketh righteousness, is accepted with him.

God loves the world and adopted us all through a promise He made Abraham, not obedience to the law of Moses

Having been in church since I was a child, I always understood that it was my duty to follow the Ten Commandments: read my Bible and pray every day so I grow.. If I didn't, that would be considered a sin, I would shrink, and I wouldn't get into heaven. Stated simply enough.

It was my job to repent and then try to better myself by continually realizing that I am still a sinner, but saved by grace, and God is merciful to my unrighteousness and renews that mercy every morning. It can be overwhelming to try and please God with my repentance and please my family and friends at the same time because sometimes the two things, God and friends, don't overlap as well as I would like.

I look up to Joshua, Aaron and Moses because they were great leaders that God led through the wilderness. They stood firm with God and committed themselves even in the hardships and trials of 40 years wandering in the wilderness! I don't want to break a commandment in my wilderness journey because it may turn a 13 day trip into a 40 year excursion There's also, of course, Jesus in the New Testament, who forgave all of my sins so I could have a chance at redemption. I don't want to die until after I have confessed my latest sin and repented. This way I can be sure to make it to heaven.

Based on all these thoughts about following God growing up in the Church, it seemed God only moved through my internal remorse, and display of said remorse (my confession of sins), when I repented.

In 2001, I was in an car accident. I was in a coma for approximately 6 weeks and then a few more weekd in rehabilitation. While in rehab, I had 2 ½ - 3 months to just lay in bed and reflect on my life. I thought about how I got to this place, wondered if was supposed to learn something from this and how I'm going to change my life from this point forward. Laying in bed all day might sound like a nice reprieve from my troubles, but are clear reasons why you shouldn't have a love for sleep. Sleep isn't fulfilling unless it is earned.

In the beginning, I had a diaper that had to be changed. I then had to wait on a nurse to find time to come and transition me to my wheelchair so I could use the bathroom. They had to accompany me to the toilet make sure I didn't fall over on the stool. Yeah, a little embarrassing don't you think? They had to help me in the shower too. I had to be watched at all times because I was at risk of falling or injuring myself. I made one attempt to go to the bathroom by myself and I was found keeled over on the floor. So aside from bathroom breaks, laying in bed and going through physical therapy, nothing else was happening, aside from my thoughts racing all day, every day.

I remember thinking about how I didn't deserve God to heal me because of all the bad stuff I had done. The accumulation of sins is a sure way to develop mental disqualification. I had grown up in church and was always conscious of God, but I didn't follow the commandments, so I wondered how God was going to move in my life. Then, as I was on my hospital bed, I found this verse: 2 Peter 1:3…

"According as his divine power hath given unto us all things that pertain unto life and godliness, through the knowledge of him that hath called us to glory and virtue."

I'm sorry, what? I don't have to ask God for anything because He has already given it all to me? By His divine power, he's given us all things? This messed with my meekness theology. I thought Christians were supposed to be lowly souls that didn't have possession. I mean yeah, God could bless me if "I did everything right," but it shouldn't be my goal. I shouldn't just be a rule follower, I should strive to be a martyr! My goal should be to sell everything and follow God: an allegory for all believers. Right? I had never been told that I already had everything.

This changed my perspective a little bit. I went from a mindset of trying to do things to earn God's approval and blessing to knowing I could do and have all things. Some things take a little more patience and time to see their fruit in my life. When a fruit seed is planted it doesn't grow and produce fruit over night because there hasn't been time for the fruit to develop.

…neither shall your vine cast her fruit before the time in the field…- Malachi 3:11

I wish I could say that I started walking in like 2 days, but I didn't start walking unassisted until a week before I left in-patient therapy.

The mindset of having all things has followed me to this day. I can't say it has always been prevalent and I have encountered a few difficulties and still have things I deal with. The one place I have noticed the most change is in how I see God. I was a scared Christian, always afraid I was going to mess up and that my momentary unrighteousness would allow the devil to steal, kill and destroy my life and I might end up in the hospital again… only the next time I may not be so lucky. Now, this verse in 2 Peter 1:3 helps me see God in a brand new light: branded by God…. You might say

Good intentions?

I feel like I have been lied to as a Christian. I don't believe it was intentional, but I can understand why people get so upset when they look to Christians to be "a light in a dark world." Christians can sometimes be so bright to those they are trying to help by being that light to the world that people respond by throwing some shade to protect themselves. While Christians are trying to preserve life and bring more taste to the world by being the salt of the earth, they can overdo it and it leaves a really salty taste in a person's mouth. Now, their response to Christianity becomes salty.

I believe that most pastors are what the Bible calls "vain janglers" or empty talkers. See what 1 Timothy 1 says about this:

1 Timothy 1

6 From which some having swerved have turned aside unto vain jangling;
7 Desiring to be teachers of the law; understanding neither what they say, nor whereof they affirm."

See also what's written in 2 Corinthians 3:15, where it says, "But even unto this day, when Moses is read, the vail is upon their heart."

It's for these reasons that my Christianity at one time, as well as many other Christians, fell under the theology of "meek and weak" Christianity instead of what's written in 2 Peter 1:3. I am not saying that we are to forget the law, but the law has been completed. When a believer tries to be justified, or be righteous, by the Law, they fall from grace. See what it says in Galatians:

"Christ has become of no effect unto you, whosoever of you is justified by the law; ye have fallen from grace." - Galatians 5:4

But, Jesus says that the two most important laws are to love God and love you neighbors.

Mark 12:30-31

30 And thou shalt love the Lord thy God with all thy heart, and with all thy soul, and with all thy mind, and with all thy strength: this is the first commandment.

31 And the second is like, namely this, Thou shalt love thy neighbour as thyself. There is none other commandment greater than these.

These are great goals to have but can not be fulfilled in the flesh unless you are led by the Spirit. If you are a believer you are filled with the Spirit of God because you are righteous: it's a gift..

The law Isn't for a righteous man, but is for a certain type of man. It's for men and women who are lawless and disobedient and unholy. . See how 1 Timothy 1 puts it:

"9 Knowing this, that the law is not made for a righteous man, but for the lawless and disobedient, for the ungodly and for sinners, for unholy and profane, for murderers of fathers and murderers of mothers, for manslayers, 10 For whoremongers, for them that defile themselves with mankind, for menstealers, for liars, for perjured persons, and if there be any other thing that is contrary to sound doctrine." – 1 Timothy 1

24 Wherefore the law was our schoolmaster to bring us unto Christ, that we might be justified by faith. -Galatians 3:24

I'm going to add another interesting fact about the biblical law. The law of Moses came from the priesthood of Aaron, but Christ is a new High Priest. We are no longer to look to Moses for direction. Moses was only a servant, but Jesus is Lord.

"It is not this way for My servant Moses; He is faithful in all My household." - Numbers 12:7

"…nor the servant above his lord." - Matthew 10:24

"For the priesthood being changed, there is made of necessity a change also of the law." - Hebrews 7:12

We no longer follow priests made after a carnal commandment, but we follow a priest made after an oath and the power of an endless life.

"15 And it is yet far more evident: for that after the similitude of Melchisedec there ariseth another priest, 16 Who is made, not after the law of a carnal commandment, but after the power of an endless life." – Hebrews 7:15-16

This is His Commandment…

"This is my commandment, That ye love one another, as I have loved you." – John 15:12

Jesus loved through the Spirit of God and not as Himself. The Holy Ghost descended in a bodily shape like a dove upon him, and a voice came from heaven, which said, Thou art my beloved Son; in the I am well pleased. – Matthew 3:16-17

These are the fruits of the Holy Spirit, (ghost) as stated in Galatians 5:22-23.

"22 But the fruit of the Spirit is love, joy, peace, longsuffering, gentleness, goodness, faith, 23 Meekness, temperance: against such there is no law."

If there is no law under this New Priesthood then what can I be accused of? Who can even accuse me? As it says in John 12:31, "Now is the time for judgment on this world; now the prince of this world will be driven out."

If the prince of the world has been cast out, I, a Gentile, can only excuse or accuse myself.

"Indeed, when Gentiles, who do not have the law, do by nature things required by the law, they are a law for themselves, even though they do not have the law." – Romans 2:14

Anybody who tells you differently is trying to control you.

Our fight is with our flesh, who is the devil. Our flesh is where the seed of satan: sin, lives. Sin came into the world and everything is made from the world and has sin in it. The Bible says, "the rock will cry out if my people don't worship Me", God will be granted His due praise with or without disciples. Interesting, and funny enough, the Matrix is a great example of that verse. How amusing is it that Hollywood could tell the story of truth, while the church is getting it so wrong. Most of the Church seems to be worried about what Moses wrote in his hundreds of laws after the Ten Commandments, but God is concerned with what he wrote on our minds and hearts. See what it says in Hebrews 8:7-10:

"7 For if that first covenant had been faultless, then should no place have been sought for the second. 8 For finding fault with them, he saith, Behold, the days come, saith the Lord, when I will make a new covenant with the house of Israel and with the house of Judah: 9 Not according to the covenant that I made with their fathers in the day when I took them by the hand to lead them out of the land of Egypt; because they continued not in my covenant, and I regarded them not, saith the Lord. 10 For this is the covenant that I will make with the house of Israel after those days, saith the Lord; I will put my laws into their mind, and write them in their hearts: and I will be to them a God, and they shall be to me a people."

The law of Moses has been fulfilled and now all are included in the house of Israel. Stop listening to religion that tells you that you are a sinner saved by grace, because you are the Righteousness of God and you need to start acting like it.

SPIRIT or BEHAVIOR

"24 God is a Spirit: and they that worship him must worship him in spirit and in truth." – John 4:24

Now there's another cultural proclamation in Christianity today that isn't totally accurate. We have an understanding that there is a Spiritual realm, and people believe that there are demons and angels fighting each other for the salvation of our souls. While there is some truth to this, I do believe that too much focus is placed on spiritual battles and not enough value placed on our victory in Christ

God is a Spirit. What does that mean? Here's the Biblical definition according to Outline of Biblical Usage:

G4151

Spirit – the third person of the triune God, the Holy Spirit, coequal, coeternal with the Father and the Son

- Sometimes referred to in a way which emphasizes his personality and character (the "Holy" Spirit)

- Sometimes referred to in a way which emphasizes his work and power (the Spirit of "Truth")

It's never referred to as a depersonalized force.

The spirit, (i.e. the vital principle by which the body is animated), the rational spirit, the power by which the human being feels, thinks, decides

The soul, a spirit (i.e. a simple essence), devoid of all or at least all grosser matter, and possessed of the power of knowing, desiring, deciding, and acting

A life giving spirit

A human soul that has left the body

A spirit higher than man but lower than God, i.e. an angel

Used of demons, or evil spirits, who were conceived as inhabiting the bodies of men

The spiritual nature of Christ, higher than the highest angels and equal to God, the divine nature of Christ

The disposition or influence which fills and governs the soul of any one

The efficient source of any power, affection, emotion, desire, etc.

A movement of air (a gentle blast)

Of the wind, hence the wind itself

Breath of nostrils or mouth

The first explanation say, "The third person of the triune God, the Holy Spirit, coequal, coeternal with the Father and the Son", and has to do with personality, character, work and power of an emphasis on these characteristics. The third definition of the 1st subset says "never referred to as a depersonalized force" A common definition online of "Spirit" is defined, "depersonalized as divest of human characteristics or individuality."

So it could read something like "never separate from human characteristics." These characteristics can always be attributed to the person. Philippians 4:13 helps us see this connection between human characteristics and spirituality by saying, "I can do all things through [a]Christ who strengthens me." The word, Christ, is also translated as "Him who". Christ does this through my human characteristics, but only because the "Spirit", or behavior of Christ, empowers me to do them. My flesh is weak, too weak to perform them. I am empowered to prosper, not possessed to. The spirit isn't some outside force that's pushing me uncontrollably to do what I don't want to or can't do! The power is given to me through Christ's behavior, His Spirit, that's put into my mind and written into my heart, just as Hebrews 8 stated!

The Second definition says the spirit, i.e. the vital principal by which the body is animated.

The rational spirit, the power by which the human being feels, thinks, decides

The soul

While I don't believe the spirit of a man is the same as his soul, I do believe that people can be spirited. Spirited is defined by the Oxford Dictionary as, "full of energy, enthusiasm, and determination" or "having a specified character, outlook on life, or mood."

This is why Alcohol is called "spirits" because it makes you spirited but that spirit, behavior, is motivated by alcohol. You can be empowered with, or have the spirit of, Joy, Power or Faith, but you can also be empowered, or have the spirit, of fear, murder or division. What you surround yourself with or consume helps you determine your spiritual well-being. Again, this isn't some uncontrollable realm we face.

The third biblical definition says spirit, i.e. a simple essence, devoid of all or at least all grosser matter, and possessed of the power of knowing, desiring, deciding, and acting

A life giving spirit

A human soul that has left the body

A spirit higher than man but lower than God, i.e. an angel

Used of demons, or evil spirits, who were conceived as inhabiting the bodies of men

The Spirit is life. This doesn't mean it makes your heart beat or your lungs breathe oxygen, but what it does mean is that it is what animates your behaviors. It's the reason why you do things. Your "spirit" is possessed by the power of knowing, desiring, deciding and acting. It is what activates the pursuit of life.

The 3rd bullet point says the spirit is higher than man, but lower than God. It gives an example of angels and demons, since they are supposedly fallen angels (based on tradition and not scripture). That is a false teaching that man, the species, is lower than angels and demons. We, men and women are gods, but not Gods. David is the first to bring this up.

"I have said, 'Ye are gods; and all of you are children of the most High.'" – Psalms 82:6

Then Jesus quotes David later in the Gospels…

Jesus answered them, "Is it not written in your Law, 'I have said you are "gods"'? – John 10:34

The word "gods" in John 10:34 is G2316 and means theos and is a general name for a deity, but the original scripture Jesus is referring to is the one from Psalms 82:6. "God" from Psalm 82:6 is the word h430 and is the Hebrew word ʻĕlōhîm. This word is the same word for God, but we are gods, children of the Most High God.

Strongholds

The next time you have a thought or vain imagination: some people call these demons, that needs to be cast down. Just ask yourself, "who told you that?" The same question God asked Adam in The Garden in Genesis. It wasn't because God didn't know. It was because Adam was listening to something he was supposed to rule over. In our case, it is our own flesh that deceives.

"27 But I keep under my body, and bring it into subjection: lest that by any means*, when I have preached to others, I myself should be a castaway." – 1 Corinthians 9

Number 4 bullet point in the definition of spirit says, "the disposition or influence which fills and governs the soul of any one" and is described as the efficient source of any power, affection, emotion and desire. A spirit is your motivation and not something that possesses you. You could appear to be possessed based on how motivated you are, like it's some unnatural sensation because it happens so infrequently, but it is not something you can't control. You have the power.

Point number 5 of G4151 says, "a movement of air, a gentle blast," and is a reference to God breathing life into Adam. The Spirit, or behavior, of God is the only Spirit a believer should be concerned with.

"This then is the message which we have heard of Him, and declare unto you, that God is light, and in him is no darkness at all." – 1 John 1:5

God is spirit (John 4:24) and God is light. This would make the Spirit light and there is no darkness in it. We move from the kingdom of darkness into the kingdom of light. As it's stated in John 8:12 (and more verses throughout the bible),

Be the light

"Then spake Jesus again unto them, saying, I am the light of the world: he that followeth me shall not walk in darkness, but shall have the light of life."

"Who hath delivered us from the power of darkness, and hath translated us into the kingdom of his dear Son (light):" – Colossians 1:13

"But if we walk in the light, as he is in the light, we have fellowship with one another, and the blood of Jesus, his Son, purifies us from all sin." – 1 John 1:7

Preaching that darkness has power is opposed to what the Bible says because we see there is no darkness in the spirit and therefore no darkness or power of darkness in the spirit. Darkness is just the absence of light.

So if we are walking in the light of the Spirit and we mess up, what would we be walking in if it isn't the darkness of the spirit? It's the flesh!

"For the flesh lusteth against the Spirit, and the Spirit against the flesh: and these are contrary the one to the other: so that ye cannot do the things that ye would." – Galatians 5:17

While I did not find any verses about fighting spiritual darkness, I do find this verse about the spirit fighting the flesh. Why would the spirit fight the flesh? For a reference,, these are the things the flesh wants us to do as referenced in Galatians 5:19-21:

"...Adultery, fornication, uncleanness, lasciviousness, 20 Idolatry, witchcraft, hatred, variance, emulations, wrath, strife, seditions, heresies, 21 Envyings, murders, drunkenness, revellings, and such like..."

These attributes would be from the kingdom of darkness or the absence of light

"So then they that are in the flesh cannot please God." – Romans 8:8

I have been taught my whole life that these works break the commandments and allow sin in my life. Satan can then go before God and accuse me of that sin and this would disqualify me from the blessing in my life. I believed this until recently. I stopped trying to keep the 10 commandments. I am instead led by the Spirit of God and only try to produce fruit that is Spirit lead. If you're unaware of what I mean by "producing fruits of the Spirit", here's the list found in Galatians 4:22-23,

"22 But the fruit of the Spirit is love, joy, peace, longsuffering, gentleness, goodness, faith, 23 Meekness, temperance: against such there is no law."

I follow the principles of the fruits of the Spirit because...

"... the righteousness of the law might be fulfilled in us, who walk not after the flesh, but after the Spirit." – Romans 8:4

Besides, we, Americans, are what the Bible considers Gentiles and have never been under the Law of Moses. Therefore, Satan could not and will not ever accuse any person who is not from the nation of Israel of not following the law of Moses. Yes, the Bible calls him, satan, the accuser of the brethren? Brethren is a reference to others of Jewish descent. It does not say he is the accuser of the neighbors, which are what non-Jews are in Biblical terms.

Abraham

This whole thing can be traced back to Abraham and Sarah, who despite what their bodies told them, believed God and his promise about a seed, who is Jesus. His promise that all nations would be blessed and not just the nation of Israel: neighbors and brethren. As Acts 10 says…

"But in every nation he that feareth him, and worketh righteousness, is accepted with him." – Acts 10:35

Satan is no longer able to accuse anyone of breaking the law of Moses and has never been able to accuse a gentile. The law has been fulfilled and he, satan, no longer has authority

"Now is the judgment of this world: now shall the prince of this world be cast out." – John 12:31

The issue we face now isn't Satan but his seed: sin.

"Wherefore, as by one man sin entered into the world, and death by sin; and so death passed upon all men, for that all have sinned." – Romans 5:12

But don't worry because…

"Ye are of God, little children, and have overcome them: because greater is he that is in you, than he that is in the world." – 1 John 4:4

I write all this not to edify myself, but because I want you to know the Truth. Here's more knowledge bombs from Hebrews.

"8Though he were a Son, yet learned he obedience by the things which he suffered; 9And being made perfect, he became the author of eternal salvation unto all them that obey him; 10Called of God an high priest after the order of Melchisedec. 11Of whom we have many things to say, and hard to be uttered, seeing ye are dull of hearing. 12For when for the time ye ought to be teachers, ye have need that one teach you again which be the first principles of the oracles of God; and are become such as have need of milk, and not of strong meat. 13For every one that useth milk is unskilful in the word of righteousness: for he is a babe. 14But strong meat belongeth to them that are of full age, even those who by reason of use have their senses exercised to discern both good and evil." – Hebrews 5:8-14

I have always heard the last part of this scripture in the context of eating spiritual food because that is what Jesus ate and this is where we should get our nourishment. I read the verses before and the seemingly common understanding is not contextual.

Verse 8 the word "Son" is talking about Jesus, because of the capitalized "S", and tells us He learned his obedience by the things by which he suffered. This is a revelation. Growing up, I always heard that we were to "cast our sufferings into the sea." Jesus died so that we wouldn't have to suffer. It was our right and authority and the mountains in our lives would have to listen to our words when they lined up with scripture. When the mountains wouldn't listen though, there was always an unspoken understanding that I needed to have more faith. I would get this faith by hearing, and hearing the word of God. For my donation of 150 dollars, I could get a tape series that teaches me all about getting more faith.

I needed to get the sin out of my life to hear more clearly from God! I could stop sinning by following the Law of Moses because it is sin that breaks the commandments. That would just heap more guilt and shame on top of the burden of not being able to complete the law. I needed more faith so I could more adequately listen to the Word, but as soon as I broke the Law of Moses, that faith would go away because I had let sin into my life.

This was an avenue the devil could steal, kill and destroy, but I needed the faith that I had lost to keep that from happening. Christianity isn't this light and easy yoke Jesus had promised because there are so many subtle nuances you have to adhere to. You might become an outcast to the popular "Holy" Christian circles, and not necessarily Christ, if you do not adhere to the unspoken commandments. Koinonia, the Hebrew word for "fellowship," is what connects us all in our quest to be Holy like He is Holy. So most follow the man-made laws so that they can be accepted, but in their quest for acceptance, they end up selling their souls. It's Sadd u cee (haha)?

Christ is called to be a High priest, but not in the same fashion as those with infirmities, sin, in their flesh, but after the power of an endless life.

"Who is made, not after the law of a carnal commandment, but after the power of an endless life." – Hebrews 7:16

If the law of Moses was good, why would we need to change it and if we do change it, would it just be more of the same?? Hebrews asks the same question.

"If therefore perfection were by the Levitical priesthood, (for under it the people received the law,) what further need was there that another priest should rise after the order of Melchisedec, and not be called after the order of Aaron?" - Hebrews 7:11

Well it's because…

"And it is yet far more evident: for that after the similitude of Melchisedec there ariseth another priest." – Hebrews 7:15

This priest was first introduced in Genesis 14

"18 And Melchizedek king of Salem brought forth bread and wine: and he was the priest of the most high God. 19 And he blessed him, and said, Blessed be Abram of the most high God, possessor of heaven and earth: 20 And blessed be the most high God, which hath delivered thine enemies into thy hand. And he gave him tithes of all." – Genesis 14:18-20

Now if we cross reference this scripture with the new testament scriptures, we can see that this King of Peace is a type of Jesus. See what's written here in Matthew:

"26While they were eating, Jesus took bread, and when he had given thanks, he broke it and gave it to his disciples, saying, "Take and eat; this is my body." 27 Then he took a cup, and when he had given thanks, he gave it to them, saying, "Drink from it, all of you. 28 This is my blood of the covenant, which is poured out for many for the forgiveness of sins." – Matthew 26:26-28

Melchizdeck provided the sacraments for communion in Genesis 1:18 and Jesus did the same thing following the lineage of his priesthood.

The Bible said Abraham gave tithes. The law of Moses had not been written yet, but Abraham set the precedent of tithing. Tithing isn't an old covenant thing because it was first introduced by Abram. He planted a seed by giving to the Priest of the Most High God: Melchizedek. That seed was blessed and multiplied but only after Abraham was tempted by God.

And it came to pass after these things, that God did tempt Abraham, and said unto him, Abraham: and he said, Behold, here I am. Genesis 22:1

We know that God doesn't tempt people (James 1:13). The word "tempted" means:

To test, try, prove, tempt, assay, put to the proof or test

This word was translated as "prove" twenty other times in the King James Version. This, I believe, is an example of God chastising the ones He loves. This is what God said after Abraham proved himself faithful:

17 That in blessing I will bless thee, and in multiplying I will multiply thy seed as the stars of the heaven, and as the sand which is upon the sea shore; and thy seed shall possess the gate of his enemies; 18 And in thy seed shall all the nations of the earth be blessed; because thou hast obeyed my voice. – Genesis 22:17-18

Because Abraham believed God more than what his circumstances told him, we have all been blessed. Abraham didn't fight the devil or satan, he didn't put on his spiritual armor and he didn't have a Bible reading plan. All he did was believe in God.

I feel like most "Christians" could relate to these scripture in John 9:27-29:

"27 He answered them, I have told you already, and ye did not hear: wherefore would ye hear it again? Will ye also be his disciples (the disciples inviting religious leaders to follow Jesus)? 28 Then they reviled him, and said, Thou art his disciple; but we are Moses' disciples. 29 We know that God spake unto Moses: as for this fellow (Jesus), we know not from whence he is."

It seems that the law of Moses is put upon a pedestal because Jesus, acting as a Rabi and talking to Jews, said the two most important commandments are to love God and to love people. Here's your reminder about where this is in the Bible:

"36 Master, which is the great commandment in the law? 37 Jesus said unto him, Thou shalt love the Lord thy God with all thy heart, and with all thy soul, and with all thy mind. 38 This is the first and great commandment. 39 And the second is like unto it, Thou shalt love thy neighbour as thyself. 40 On these two commandments hang all the law and the prophets." – Matthew 22:26-40

In reality, Jesus, as a High Priest in the order of Melchizedek, gave one commandment and that is to love like He loves (John 15:12). Let's investigate further.

"15 And it is yet far more evident: for that after the similitude of Melchisedec there ariseth another priest, 16 Who is made, not after the law of a carnal commandment, but after the power of an endless life." – Hebrews 7:15-16

Are you His disciple or a disciple of Moses? Seeing that you are dull of hearing, as scripture says, I believe you're a disciple of Jesus and you are blessed through Abraham by Melchizedek.

Consider then how great this Melchizedek was, even Abraham, the great patriarch of Israel, recognized this by giving him a tenth of what he had taken in battle. Now the law of Moses required that the priests, who are descendants of Levi, must collect a tithe from the rest of the people of

Israel, who are also descendants of Abraham. But Melchizedek, who was not a descendant of Levi, collected a tenth from Abraham. Melchizedek placed a blessing upon Abraham, the one who had already received the promises of God. And without question, the person who has the power to give a blessing is greater than the one who is blessed. – Hebrews 7:4-7 NLT

Work like Abraham

"….If ye were Abraham's children, ye would do the works of Abraham." – John 8:39

Stop trying to twist God's arm through obeying the law of Moses because it was never a covenant with non-Israelites! Truly follow Jesus and follow His commandment. This commandment is not a Levitical law, but comes from a High Priest in the order of Melchizedek from the tribe of Judah. Moses knew nothing about these people. God didn't use a law to bless you because He blesses us through an oath

"18 For there is verily a disannulling of the commandment going before for the weakness and unprofitableness thereof. 19 For the law made nothing perfect, but the bringing in of a better hope did; by the which we draw nigh unto God. 20 And inasmuch as not without an oath he was made priest." – Hebrews 7:18-20

"The LORD hath sworn, and will not repent, Thou art a priest for ever after the order of Melchizedek." – Psalm 110:4

How did Jesus love if it wasn't as himself? Following the connecting narrative in the scriptures below.

"And the Holy Ghost descended in a bodily shape like a dove upon him, and a voice came from heaven, which said, Thou art my beloved Son; in thee I am pleased." - Mark 3:22

These are the fruits of the Spirit…

"22But the fruit of the Spirit is love, joy, peace, patience, kindness, goodness, faithfulness, 23gentleness, and self-control. Against such things there is no law." – Galatians 5:22-23

"This I say then, Walk in the Spirit, and ye shall not fulfil the lust of the flesh." – Galatians 5:16

"But every man is tempted, when he is drawn away of his own lust, and enticed. Then when lust hath conceived, it bringeth forth sin: and sin, when it is finished, bringeth forth death." – James 1:14-15

What kind of lusts are men tempted with?

"19 Now the works of the flesh are manifest, which are these; Adultery, fornication, uncleanness, lasciviousness, 20 Idolatry, witchcraft, hatred, variance, emulations, wrath, strife, seditions, heresies, 21 Envyings, murders, drunkenness, revellings, and such like: of the which I tell you before, as I have also told you in time past, that they which do such things shall not inherit the kingdom of God." – Galatians 5

One of the ways to not give in to these temptations is to follow the law of Moses. Every time I am tempted, I can just shoulder it upon myself;"… thou shalt not…." And insert one of the works of the flesh. This is how all of the Israelites did it so it should be good enough for me? Right?

Now, forget the fact that God only made this "Law" with the Hebrews at Mt. Sinai, where a tribe of Gentiles were not present. Focus on the fact that all of mankind are sinners and need the law as a guide to keep them from sinning. This yoke of bondage is only fulfilled when all of its laws are completed, but man in the weakness of his flesh, can never fulfill the righteousness of the Law. He needs a savior to show him the way to righteousness.

The law of Moses Is also referred to as the "carnal commandments" because it attempts to give power to a person to live above their desires. Desires like…eating a half gallon of ice cream (my guilty pleasure), or that melted candy bar you left on the dash of your car, or even Netflix and chilling.

These things are not bad in themselves, but when they distract you from what God wants you to do, things start to get a little dicey. The Achilles heel of the commandment is that instead of empowering a believer to live above the desires of the flesh, it actually gives sin, in the flesh, more power. The law is spiritual: power from God, and is not able to be completed by the flesh. It's righteous requirements are a spiritual endeavor and mankind is flesh and is not able fulfill the fullness of it.

There are some, in fact most, who put the blame of all things evil on the devil because it is an easy out that doesn't require much personal responsibility. It's popular to believe the devil can roam like a lion, seeking whom he can steal, kill and destroy. Then, if something bad happens in life, it is the devil's fault! They read all of the blessing scriptures, but don't read any of the scriptures about being perplexed and crushed on every side.

We are troubled on every side, yet not distressed; we are perplexed, but not in despair; - 2 Corinthians 4:8

This believer needs to get a better handle on the words coming out of their mouth based on what we hear pastors saying. But the Bible says something different.

4 Who comforteth us in all our tribulation, that we may be able to comfort them which are in any trouble, by the comfort wherewith we ourselves are comforted of God.

5 For as the sufferings of Christ abound in us, so our consolation also aboundeth by Christ.

6 And whether we be afflicted, it is for your consolation and salvation, which is effectual in the enduring of the same sufferings which we also suffer: or whether we be comforted, it is for your consolation and salvation.

7 And our hope of you is stedfast, knowing, that as ye are partakers of the sufferings, so shall ye be also of the consolation. – 2 Corinthians

Christians seem to forget that we are to take up our cross and follow Jesus and suffer like He did. We don't even dare mention that God chastises the one He loves. Now, I am not talking about cancer or sickness or anything like that, but I am more referring to the difficult periods of life that end up being teaching moments when we reflect upon them. These are like the obstacle courses in the race of life that have to be completed to get you where you need to be. James says it best,

"2 My brethren, count it all joy when ye fall into divers temptations; 3 Knowing this, that the trying of your faith worketh patience. 4 But let patience have her perfect work, that ye may be perfect and entire, wanting nothing." – James 1:2-4

It's time to level up.

These are all great talking points, but I want to focus on the temptation of man. How is a man tempted by his flesh and not the devil? Well, the flesh and the devil are the same thing. If you didn't catch it the first time, I've written multiple times about how sin was the serpent in the garden and how the serpent is the devil. It is even scriptural and it's certainly not something I am trying to devise to make myself more appealing.

"And the great dragon was cast out, THAT OLD SERPENT, CALLED THE DEVIL, and Satan, which deceiveth the whole world: he was cast out into the earth, and his angels were cast out with him." – Revelation 12:9

The devil, sin, is the seed of the serpent that God said would be crushed by the seed of the woman: who is Jesus. These entities are also referred to as the corruptible and incorruptible seed. Lucifer was never the serpent and we can see him in the Garden not being a serpent through a verse that is commonly understood as a reference to Lucifer (Satan).

"Thou hast been in Eden the garden of God; every precious stone was thy covering…" – Ezekiel 28:13-15

He wasn't a serpent? The serpent is best understood through the Exodus of the Israelites from Egypt. They are travelling along and they make

God mad and He sends some fiery serpents to bite them. Here's where it's referenced:

"And the people spake against God, and against Moses, Wherefore have ye brought us up out of Egypt to die in the wilderness? For there is no bread, neither is there any water; and our soul loatheth this light bread. And the Lord sent fiery serpents among the people, and they bit the people; and much people of Israel died." – Numbers 21:5-6

The same word that was translated as fiery in Leviticus was translated as "Seraphim" in Isaiah.

"Above him were seraphim, each with six wings: With two wings they covered their faces, with two they covered their feet, and with two they were flying." – Isaiah 6:2

With a different understanding, it changes things a little bit. What I read now is that God sent six winged serpent angels, seraphim, to bite the Israelites. This story isn't a new one because it is just a recreation of the story told in Genesis. Now God didn't send the serpent in Genesis because the serpent, an angel, was sent by the head angel, Lucifer, to "bite" Adam and Eve so that they died "spiritually" and become sin's servants instead of God's servants.

"Don't you know that when you offer yourselves to someone as obedient slaves, you are slaves of the one you obey-whether you are slaves to sin, which leads to death, or to obedience, which leads to righteousness?" – Romans 6:16

This story sounds familiar…

"Therefore the people came to Moses and said, We have sinned, for we have spoken against the LORD, and against thee; pray unto the LORD, that he take away the serpents from us. And Moses prayed for the people. And the LORD said unto Moses, Make thee a fiery serpent, and set it upon a pole: and it shall come to pass, that every one that is bitten, when he looketh upon it, shall live." – Num 21:7-8

The people then went to Moses and asked him to go to God for them. God then instructed Moses to put a serpent on a pole and when all the people looked upon it they would be healed. This is a type and shadow of Jesus being our mediator as well as Jesus the atonement for our sin through his crucifixion on the cross. We look unto Jesus in the same fashion as the Israelites, so the bite of sin will not lead to death.

"Looking unto Jesus the author and finisher of our faith..." – Hebrews 12:2

The way this verse reads is kind of confusing because it appears to be talking about "our" faith. What makes it confusing is that the Israelites didn't have faith, as a gift, because faith was locked up under the law and the Israelites were under the law. How did we go from looking upon Jesus, which the Israelites experienced to "our faith"?

There are two types of faith; a measure that all man is born with and the "Gift of" which is without measure: this is the same faith that Jesus has. The measure of faith was used by the Israelites, I believe, to have faith in one's self to keep the law and believe that you could do it in your own strength. The faith that was locked up was the "gift of". The Israelites sin had not been atoned so God could not dwell inside of them. He, God, had to be carried in an ark that was designed by God and built by the hands of man.

The word "our" Is in italics which means it was added by the translators to try and bring more understanding. If we take the word "our" out of the sentence it reads "Looking unto Jesus the author and finisher of faith..." This indicates a paradigm change because we always hear about how we need to have faith. To show how much faith we have we can plant a seed of a thousand dollars to meet our million dollar need or any of the other feats that late night Christian tv provides us to perform. We can show how much faith we have through the amount we give and receive a replica sword of the Holy Spirit that we can hang on the wall. This will give us an opportunity to brag about what we did to get the sword. I mean tell about how God blessed us to donate.... God looks at the heart. While I believe there are some instances of spirit lead revelations on Christian tv. I also believe there are just as many, if not more, instances of manipulation in the name of God on Christian television.

Faith is not "our" work because Jesus authorizes and finishes it. You might say he is the Alpha and Omega of Faith. Creflo Dollar illustrated faith as a pipe that God's blessings flow through. I've heard it illustrated as logistics! Bing.com defines logistics as "the detailed coordination of a complex operation involving many people, facilities, or supplies." The pipe illustration is a good one because we, in essence, control the size of the pipe and what is able to come through it because they are a reflection of our beliefs.

The logistics shows that there Is a coordination aspect to faith that can only be accounted for based on what you believe. The word "believe" is the verb that helps open the door (also Jesus) for the correct people, facilities and supplies, to be provided by God so you can't boast. So the problem isn't that we don't have faith, the problem is that we don't believe that we have it. God has given us all things that pertain to life and godliness, but we get stuck at looking at how inadequate we are.

We use the law of Moses and other people's success as a marker for our success and forget that success is not based on us. True, some people have natural talents that will get them places, but those gifts were placed there by the Lord. The law of Moses has been fulfilled so that no matter how successful a person is in fulfilling it in their power, God will not notice and bless you. We think that people are more successful because they have a certain secret method that they have been blessed with. The Bible lets us know what that secret sauce is...

"I have seen something else under the sun: The race is not to the swift or the battle to the strong, nor does food come to the wise or wealth to the brilliant or favor to the learned; but time and chance happen to them all." – Ecclesiastes 9:11

It all happens through logistics. It is a combination of being in the right place at the right time. What God wants you to do is show up because He already has and is waiting for you.

It's not what I do

One might say a few things to help themselves look heavenly. Here's a few example statements: I have a Bible reading plan on my phone and I have a streak of 400 days without missing. I mow a portion of my neighbor's yard because I love my neighbor and it's really convenient for me to do. I am always dressed to impress because I am Holy and this is how I reflect my creator. God requires me to be Holy like he is. I love God and you can tell by my giving. I give to the poor through supporting different ministries that are called to minister to those types of people. I could give a list of all the things I do in the name of God to bring me… His glory. Now many of these are legitimate, but shouldn't be broadcasted.

This is what Jesus and the Bible have to say about Pharisees and Sadducees.

"These people draweth nigh unto me with their mouth, and honoureth me with their lips; but their heart is far from me." – Matthew 15:8

"And he said to them, "Well did Isaiah prophesy of you hypocrites, as it is written, "'This people honors me with their lips, but their heart is far from me;'" - Mark 7:6

"And the Lord said: "Because this people draw near with their mouth and honor me with their lips, while their hearts are far from me, and their fear of me is a commandment taught by men," – Isaiah 29:13

Don't be like these people because…

"They profess to know God, but they deny him by their works. They are detestable, disobedient, unfit for any good work." – Titus 1:16

"having the appearance of godliness, but denying its power. Avoid such people." – 2 Timothy 3:5

So, what are the works of God if it isn't the Commandments of God? I mean, people are supposed to judge you by your fruit, or works, and if we aren't reflecting what Moses taught what would it be. James 2:21 and Romans 4:2 both say that Abraham was judged by his works. So what were those works of Abraham? If we go through scripture, we can see a bunch of things that would disqualify him based on "Christian" standards. It is amusing that everyone will amen someone who compares them to "Father Abraham" because he is the father of our faith but few realize how unqualified he was. Before Abraham was considered the father of our faith, he was considered the father of his faults.

God tells Abraham…

Genesis 12:2-3 –

"2 And I will make of thee a great nation, and I will bless thee, and make thy name great; and thou shalt be a blessing:

3 And I will bless them that bless thee, and curse him that curseth thee: and in thee shall all families of the earth be blessed."

It's kind of like when we first get saved and we learn about God's love and have all these amazing feelings about God. We learn about the promises he has made to us and we then spend our Christian walk trying to recreate those feelings of the first time. When we aren't able to get in our lovely feelings, like in the beginning, we call it "cringe-y" because we are in an emotional famine. We try to go to Egypt: an allegory for sin, to provide those feelings for ourselves. While in Egypt, we say whatever we need to in order to try and feed and protect ourselves. We will then lie and deceive to try and get ahead, or at least that is what Abraham did, but God is still faithful.

Genesis 12 says…

10 Now there was a famine in the land, and Abram went down to Egypt to live there for a while because the famine was severe. 11 As he was about to enter Egypt, he said to his wife Sarai, "I know what a beautiful woman you

are. 12 When the Egyptians see you, they will say, 'This is his wife.' Then they will kill me but will let you live. 13 Say you are my sister, so that I will be treated well for your sake and my life will be spared because of you."

14 When Abram came to Egypt, the Egyptians saw that Sarai was a very beautiful woman. 15 And when Pharaoh's officials saw her, they praised her to Pharaoh, and she was taken into his palace. 16 He treated Abram well for her sake, and Abram acquired sheep and cattle, male and female donkeys, male and female servants, and camels.

17 But the Lord inflicted serious diseases on Pharaoh and his household because of Abram's wife Sarai. 18 So Pharaoh summoned Abram. "What have you done to me?" he said. "Why didn't you tell me she was your wife? 19 Why did you say, 'She is my sister,' so that I took her to be my wife? Now then, here is your wife. Take her and go!" 20 Then Pharaoh gave orders about Abram to his men, and they sent him on his way, with his wife and everything he had.

Genesis 16 also say…

1 Now Sarai Abram's wife bare him no children: and she had an handmaid, an Egyptian, whose name was Hagar.

2 And Sarai said unto Abram, Behold now, the Lord hath restrained me from bearing: I pray thee, go in unto my maid; it may be that I may obtain children by her. And Abram hearkened to the voice of Sarai.

3 And Sarai Abram's wife took Hagar her maid the Egyptian, after Abram had dwelt ten years in the land of Canaan, and gave her to her husband Abram to be his wife.

4 And he went in unto Hagar, and she conceived: and when she saw that she had conceived, her mistress was despised in her eyes.

Next thing that Abraham did that would be looked down upon in church is he committed adultery: he slept with a woman that wasn't his wife. Now, pastors use this as an example of trying to "help" God. That something bad always comes out of "helping" that wasn't expected and it usually becomes the problem that gets in the way of God's true plan. We call it what it was: adultery. We can judge this tree by its fruit and disqualify him from all sorts of things and positions because of his actions because that is how we are instructed to judge people: by their fruit.

"And Abraham said of Sarah his wife, She is my sister: and Abimelech king of Gerar sent, and took Sarah." – Genesis 20:2

Abraham tried to pass his wife off as his sister again, which she was because they both had the same father: Terah (Genesis 20:12), but failed to mention that she was his wife. The Lord moved upon the king and the king did not touch her and returned her to Abraham. Like the first king, Abraham was given more wealth and told he could stay wherever he pleased on their land.

This was Abraham's work: he believed.

"And not being weak in faith, he did not consider his own body, already dead (since he was about a hundred years old), and the deadness of Sarah's womb." – Romans 4:19

"And Abraham was a hundred years old, when his son Isaac was born unto him." – Genesis 21:5

We can see God's promise and then Abraham messing it up time and time again, but he didn't really mess up because all of this happened before the law of Moses.

"And this I say, that the covenant, that was confirmed before of God in Christ, the law, which was four hundred and thirty years after, cannot disannul, that it should make the promise of no effect." – Galatians 3:17

We aren't disqualified from God's promise either because of "sin" because our promise was before the law. We, just Like Abraham, are not under the law, and never have been. Jesus was accused of all sin on the cross so that no matter what I do, I cannot be accused. Now, I am what the Bible would consider a Gentile and Gentiles can only accuse and excuse themselves.

"14 For when the Gentiles, which have not the law, do by nature the things contained in the law, these, having not the law, are a law unto themselves: 15 Which shew the work of the law written in their hearts, their conscience also bearing witness, and their thoughts the mean while accusing or else excusing one another." – Romans 2:14-15

Abraham didn't have a mindset of disqualification. He wasn't trying to get more of anything. He believed what God said and that it would happen because He said it. Abraham didn't believe what God had promised was tied to anything that he did or didn't do and he did do some things that would have ended most marriages, but Sarah had faith to believe in God also.

"Through faith also Sara herself received strength to conceive seed, and was delivered of a child when she was past age, because she judged him faithful who had promised." – Hebrews 11:11

Neither Abraham or Sarah had a mindset of disqualification, and believed God, regardless of what their bodies told them.

We find ourselves today as spiritual descendants of Abraham wanting to inherit his promises, but not willing to do what he did. They believed, regardless of what their bodies told them, that God would do what He said He would do. What do we believe? Most Christians believe that we are to "love our neighbors as ourselves" and to "love God" because Jesus said those are the two greatest commandments. We try to qualify ourselves for God's blessing by living a Holy and Righteous life because that is what God has called us to do, but our lives are defined by Jesus' finished work, not our works. We use the law of Moses as a type of wax to buff and shine our spiritual armor. The more good we do, the brighter our armor gets and we can look into a mirror and see a reflection of ourselves…er… a..Jesus. We have become satisfied with that type of gospel because it is without spot or blemish. We have been able to move all of our mountains out of the way so we must have great faith. We can then see God's blessing in our life because of our great faith through all the blessings and prosperity bestowed upon us. We have arrived, or that is what I believe most Christians are looking into the face of Jesus for.

Get better not bitter

Bruce Lee has a quote that speaks profoundly towards this issue, "Don't pray for an easy life, pray for the strength to endure a difficult one." I am sure there are many other people that have said something similar in different ways. This quote seems to go against the Christian faith because, as Christians, we are supposed to speak to our problems so like the mountain they are, they can be removed and cast into the sea. At least that is the way the gospel has been presented my whole life.

There has always been an underlying theme that if you have problems, it is because you are in sin and don't have enough faith. We are not doing enough good works so that God's righteousness can be released into our lives. We hope that we have done enough and come back to get our weekly fix of hope to make it until next week so that we can, hopefully, speak to the mountains and tell them to be removed into the sea: the living water.

Removed is Strongs G142 and means according to the outline biblical usage:

To raise up, elevate, lift up

To raise from the ground, take up: stones

To raise upwards, elevate, lift up: the hand

To draw up: a fish

To take upon one's self and carry what has been raised up, to bear

To bear away what has been raised, carry off

To move from its place

To take off or away what is attached to anything

To remove

To carry off, carry away with one

To appropriate what is taken

To take away from another what is his or what is committed to him, to take by force

To take and apply to any use

To take from among the living, either by a natural death, or by violence

Cause to cease

Strongs defines it as αἴρω aírō, (ah'-ee-ro) a primary root; to lift up; by implication, to take up or away. Figuratively, to raise (the voice), keep in suspense (the mind), specially, to sail away (i.e. weigh anchor). By Hebraism (compare H5375) to expiate sin:—away with, bear (up), carry, lift up, loose, make to doubt, put away, remove, take (away, up).

"For verily I say unto you, That whosoever shall say unto this mountain, Be thou removed, and be thou cast into the sea; and shall not doubt in his heart, but shall believe that those things which he saith shall come to pass; he shall have whatsoever he saith." – Mark 11:23

Removed is Strongs number Strongs G142 and while it was translated as remove at least one time it was most often translated as take up 32 times in the KJV. It was translated as remove only 1 time out of 8 other miscellaneous words.

Some of the verses that help illustrate what I believe was the true intent of G142.

"But that ye may know that the Son of man hath power on earth to forgive sins, (then saith he to the sick of the palsy,) Arise, take up G142 thy bed, and go unto thine house." – Mat 9:6

"Then said Jesus unto his disciples, If any man will come after me, let him deny himself, and take up G142 his cross, and follow me." – Mat 16:24

"They shall take up G142 serpents; and if they drink any deadly thing, it shall not hurt them; they shall lay hands on the sick, and they shall recover." – Mar 16:18

I now read this verse in a new light! Whoever takes up and bears their mountain and throws it into the sea, and as long as they don't pick the mountain back up, whatever they are saying and believing shall come to pass.

The word "sea" Is not really defined as a literal sea and could be used metaphorically as the Mediterranean or Red Sea. The Red Sea is a great allegory for washing away sins that you have struggled with because that is how God cleansed the Israelites of the Egyptians that were chasing them. Jesus, being known as living water, you can talk about how he washes your problems away and keeps washing until you are as white as snow. Anyways, the point I am trying to make is that we initially bear the mountain. Before you start an argument with yourself about how Jesus suffered so that we wouldn't have to, I want to tell you to stop. I know we have this perception of a perfect Jesus who washes things away and I get it. That, in my opinion, is a device of the devil to keep you from becoming what you already are. Jesus suffered and suffered a lot and he did it so that our lives would be perfect. The word "perfect" doesn't mean "without trial". The word "perfect" in the Bible means "complete or mature." Jesus even speaks to this when He says, "It is finished," on the cross. Of course, I have some scripture to back this up.

"Consider it pure joy, my brothers and sisters, whenever you face trials of many kinds, because you know that the testing of your faith produces perseverance. Let perseverance finish its work so that you may be mature and complete, not lacking anything." – James 1:2-4

"Beloved, do not think it strange concerning the fiery trial which is to try you, as though some strange thing happened to you; but rejoice to the extent that you partake of Christ's sufferings, that when His glory is revealed, you may also be glad with exceeding joy. If you are reproached for the name of Christ, blessed are you, for the Spirit of glory and of God rests upon you. On their part He is blasphemed, but on your part He Is glorified." – 1 Peter 4:12-14

"In this you greatly rejoice, though now for a little while, if need be, you have been grieved by various trials, that the genuineness of your faith, being much more precious than gold that perishes, though it is tested by fire, may be found to praise, honor, and glory at the revelation of Jesus Christ, whom having not seen you love. Though now you do not see Him, yet believing, you rejoice with joy inexpressible and full of glory, receiving the end of your faith—the salvation of your souls. Of this salvation the prophets have inquired and searched carefully, who prophesied of the grace that would come to you, searching what, or what manner of time, the Spirit of Christ who was in them was indicating when He testified beforehand the sufferings of Christ and the glories that would follow." – 1 Peter 1:6-11

"But may the God of all grace, who called us to His eternal glory by Christ Jesus, after you have suffered a while, perfect, establish, strengthen, and settle you. To Him be the glory and the dominion forever and ever. Amen." – 1 Peter 5:10-11

"And not only that, but we also glory in tribulations, knowing that tribulation produces perseverance;" – Romans 5:3

"For to you it has been granted on behalf of Christ, not only to believe in Him, but also to suffer for His sake," – Philippians 1:29

"Do not fear any of those things which you are about to suffer. Indeed, the devil is about to throw some of you into prison, that you may be tested, and you will have tribulation for ten days. Be faithful until death, and I will give you the crown of life." – Revelation 2:10

Jesus had a perfect life and showed us how we are to live a perfect life…. right. Just say it is written, because the devil knows more of the Bible than we do, and he has to flee. Just like the example Jesus showed us when he was tempted by the devil. Jesus also showed us how to suffer through his death and resurrection. Trials in life are not to defeat you, they are a refining fire to purify your life. Learn to suffer like Jesus suffers.

"Looking unto Jesus the author and finisher of our faith; who for the joy that was set before him endured the cross, despising the shame, and is set down at the right hand of the throne of God." – Hebrews 12:2

Jesus completed the law.

"For the life of the flesh is in the blood: and I have given it to you upon the altar to make an atonement for your souls: for it is the blood that maketh an atonement for the soul." – Leviticus 17:11

This ripped the veil in the tabernacle and released the Spirit of God into the earth because sin no longer has dominion. Now, God can live inside of a container created with His hands (man), and empower him to do what he could not before: love, joy, peace, longsuffering, gentleness, goodness, faith, meekness temperance. These are supernatural things that are above the natural ways of man: adultery, fornication, uncleanness, lasciviousness, idolatry, witchcraft, hatred, variance, emulations, wrath, strife, seditions, heresies, envyings, murders, drunkenness, revellings, and such like

The law of Moses tried to teach man to fight his natural desires in his own power and the flesh is weak so that did not work.

Hebrews 7:18-19

"18 For there is verily a disannulling of the commandment going before for the weakness and unprofitableness thereof.

19 For the law made nothing perfect, but the bringing in of a better hope did; by the which we draw nigh unto God."

"Wherefore the law was our schoolmaster to bring us unto Christ, that we might be justified by faith." – Galatians 3:24

Once again, we go down that Romans road with Romans 10…

"9 That if thou shalt confess with thy mouth the Lord Jesus, and shalt believe in thine heart that God hath raised him from the dead, thou shalt be saved.

10 For with the heart man believeth unto righteousness; and with the mouth confession is made unto salvation."

Sin is atoned forever!

Jesus offered his body and his blood, as the final sin offering for all people for all eternity. "For by one offering he has perfected forever those being sanctified." – Hebrews 10:14

Then we are sealed with the Holy Spirit.

"In whom ye also trusted, after that ye heard the word of truth, the gospel of your salvation: in whom also after that ye believed, ye were sealed with that holy Spirit of promise." – Ephesians 3:14

Because now, we are as righteous as God is.

"…. We might become the righteousness of God." – 2 Corinthians 5:21

Now with this comes all things that pertain to life and godliness and every spiritual blessing.

"According as his divine power hath given unto us all things that pertain unto life and godliness, through the knowledge of him that hath called us to glory and virtue." – 2 Peter 1:3

"Blessed be the God and Father of our Lord Jesus Christ, who has blessed us with every spiritual blessing in the heavenly places in Christ." – Ephesians 1:3

"Now I can do all things through Christ who strengthens me." – Philippians 4:13

Because Christ has already called me to walk the works he completed before the foundation of the world.

"For we are God's handiwork, created in Christ Jesus to do good works, which God prepared in advance for us to do." – Ephesians 2:10

"…although the works were finished from the foundation of the world." – Hebrews 4:2

"…the Lamb slain from the foundation of the world." – Revelation 13:8

We look unto Jesus, who is the author and finisher of our Faith (Hebrews 12:2), who showed us how to be led by the Spirit: love, joy, peace, longsuffering, gentleness, goodness, faith, meekness, temperance: against such there is no law. We look unto Abraham and Sarah who believed God despite what his body told them.

"Look to Abraham, your father, and to Sarah, who gave you birth. When I called him he was only one man, and I blessed him and made him many." – Isaiah 51:2

Paul puts it this way…

"I therefore so run, not as uncertainly; so fight I, not as one that beateth the air: But I keep under my body, and bring it into subjection: lest that by any means, when I have preached to others, I myself should be a castaway." – 1 Corinthians 9:26-27

"Casting down imaginations, and every high thing that exalteth itself against the knowledge of God, and bringing into captivity every thought to the obedience of Christ;" - 2 Corinthians 10:5

Imagination is G3053 and means according to outline of biblical usage…

A reckoning, computation

A reasoning: such as is hostile to the Christian faith

A judgment, decision: such as conscience passes

Strongs says (figuratively) reasoning (conscience, conceit):—imagination, thought.

Using scripture to define scripture the SDC (Stephen Douglas Clopton) version of 2 Corinthians 9:26-27. It would be paraphrased as this:

I know where I am going from the start and I exhaust myself, but not against an opponent from my imagination. I dominate my body and wear myself out by making it do what I want it to do so that my testimony will lead others to Christ

This is the Spirit: love, joy, peace, longsuffering, gentleness, goodness, faith, meekness, temperance, versus the flesh: adultery, fornication, uncleanness, lasciviousness, idolatry, witchcraft, hatred, variance, emulations, wrath, strife, seditions, heresies, envyings, murders, drunkenness, revellings, and such like.

"For the flesh lusteth against the Spirit, and the Spirit against the flesh: and these are contrary one to the other: so that ye cannot do the things that ye would." – Galatians 5:17

"For all the law is fulfilled in one word, even in this; Thou shalt love thy neighbour as thyself. But if ye bite and devour one another, take heed that ye be not consumed by one of another." – Galatians 5:14-15

"Let us therefore, as many as be perfect, be thus minded: and if in any thing ye be otherwise minded, God shall reveal even this unto you." – Philippians 3:15

Heavy.

The Apostle of John is heavy, heavy in the sense that the content is dense and full of nutrition for the soul. It is not one of the synoptic gospels and can be uneasy on a person's soul because there isn't a chance to hear the information from a 2nd or 3rd perspective. There is so much to unpack that hasn't been and needs to be to get to where we are going.

I want to focus on John 8 and 9. John starts with the woman caught in adultery and Jesus writes something in the dirt and tells her accusers to cast the first stone if they are without sin. They all eventually walked away and Jesus asked the woman where her accusers were and He said, "neither do I accuser you" and told her to go and sin no more. We all have been conditioned, almost classically, that it means those in glass houses shouldn't throw stones. Jesus seems to expound on this lesson when he tells his disciples not to worry about the splinter in their neighbors eye when the have a plank in their own (Mathew 7:2). We are able to find this truth supported in many other scriptures so it must be a gospel truth, but is it?

What did Jesus write in the dirt? I have heard some say it was a list of sins of her accusers, or maybe not, no one knows with any certainty. The text has been used to drive many sermons home about Jesus knowing all that you do in secret and making a list. No need to check it twice!

You know, the fire and brimstone preaching that will scare the hell out of you? I don't believe that is literally true, or contextually true. I do find it interesting that Jesus wrote in the dirt because man was created from dirt. He might have been using it as an object lesson of types to help them remember where they came from. There is no certainty, but what I can say is the fact he wrote in the dirt speaks volumes. Everything was created from the dust of the world after it was spoken into existence. He could have been telling them they were basic? They could have had a different understanding of scripture than we do because it was written in their native tongue. Whatever the reason was, I think it received its intended response.

"He that is without sin among you, let him first cast a stone at her", this statement of Jesus is where the confusion comes in. Adultery was punishable by death under the Law of Moses (Lev 20:10, Deut 22:22-24), so one could feel safe in assuming Jesus was referring to that, but that isn't the way the sentence is set up. Jesus' predicate to casting a stone is to be without sin. That's why some people assume that Jesus wrote a list of sins of the accusers and Jesus was using that as a point of reference for His statement of "He that is without sin" on. That would make sense because all have sinned and fallen short, but sin is a noun: a person, place or thing. The phrase "without sin" is an adjective to describe a sinless person. Sin, as in the sin of the world (John 1:29), is G266 and is a noun. Why would this resonate with the accusers and why did Jesus set himself apart from those accusers by saying "neither do I accuse you?" What did the religious accusers understand that we don't? We should start in the beginning.

When we go back to the story of creation, we can imagine a world where plants and animals seem to appear after God speaks them into existence. It's an example of the power of our words in action and we too can speak things into existence.

And then we read a scripture like this onem, Hebrews 4:3…

"For we which have believed do enter into rest, as he said, As I have sworn in my wrath, if they shall enter into my rest: although the works were finished from the foundation of the world."

It Is confusing because it is hard to grasp the concept of finished before created. We can find scripture that helps explain this concept further/.

"Through faith we understand that the worlds were framed by the word of God, so that things which are seen were not made of things which do appear." – Hebrews 11:3

God could not have created the world and all that inhabits it without first framing it in faith because things that are seen are created by things we don't see.

The Message Bible says It this way…

"By faith, we see the world called into existence by God's word, what we see created by what we don't see." – Hebrews 11:3

That's what we see happening in the beginning when God spoke it and saw that it was good and blessed it. Then he creates it all out of the ground of the earth.

Here's Genesis 2: 9 & 18 to provide some helpful detail…

"8 And out of the ground made the Lord God to grow every tree that is pleasant to the sight, and good for food; the tree of life also in the midst of the garden, and the tree of knowledge of good and evil.

19 And out of the ground the Lord God formed every beast of the field, and every fowl of the air; and brought them unto Adam to see what he would call them: and whatsoever Adam called every living creature, that was the name thereof."

We can see this same series of events in the creation of man…

"So God created man in his own image, in the image of God created him; male and female created him." – Genesis 1:27

This verse is great because it sets up an explanation to parts of the story later, but man was created both male and female and then in Genesis 2, God made man a body out of the dust.

"And the Lord God formed man of the dust of the ground, and breathed into his nostrils the breath of life; and man became a living soul." – Genesis 2:7

God first created Adam and then formed him. God then breathed into Adam to give him life. We get this picture of God standing over Adam giving him CPR to try to bring him to life. While the image may be humorous, it isn't exactly what happened. When it says, "God breathed into Adam," He, God, was actually giving part of Himself to Adam. God lost part of His own life so that we could live and have life (pause to let that settle in). I say that because breathe is H5301 and the outline of biblical usage says:

To breathe, blow, sniff at, seethe, give up or lose (life)

(Qal) to breathe, blow

(Pual) to be blown

(Hiphil) to cause to breathe out

And Strongs definition says:

A primitive root; to puff, in various applications (literally, to inflate, blow hard, scatter, kindle, expire; figuratively, to disesteem):—blow, breath, give up, cause to lose (life), seething, snuff.

Adam then named all of the trees (plants) that were good for food and pleasant to sight the Lord had caused to grow out of the ground (Genesis 2:7). God then put Adam in the Garden to care for it and pointed out the Tree of the Knowledge of Good and Evil and told him not to eat of it because surely he would die (Genesis 2:17). God seeing himself in man (literally and figuratively) saw that it was not good for man to be alone and wanted to make him a help meet (Genesis 2:18)

God then made all of the beast he had created out of the ground and Adam named them but there was no help found for Adam (Genesis 2:18-20). God decided to pull from His own playbook and caused Adam to fall into a deep sleep. God took one of Adam's ribs (Genesis 2:21) and created a woman. This is where it gets a little dicey.

God gave of himself to make man in the same fashion that man, who was created male and female, was pulled from to make woman. It says God took one of man's ribs but I don't believe man had a physical body at this point. Please hear what I am saying. This word translated as rib was only translated as rib twice in Genesis. The other times H6762 it had to do with building.

Outline of Biblical Usage:

I.   Side, rib, beam

    A.   Rib (of man)

    B.   Rib (of hill, ridge, etc)

    C.   Side-chambers or cells (of temple structure)

    D.   Rib, plank, board (of cedar or fir)

    E.   Leaves (of door)

    F.   Side (of ark)

Strongs says something similar…

עֵלָצ tsêlâ', tsay-law'; or (feminine) הָעְלַצ tsal'âh; from H6760; a rib (as curved), literally (of the body) or figuratively (of a door, i.e. leaf); hence, a side, literally (of a person) or figuratively (of an object or the sky, i.e. quarter); architecturally, a (especially floor or ceiling) timber or plank (single or collective, i.e. a flooring):—beam, board, chamber, corner, leaf, plank, rib, side

Why do I go through all of this trouble? The Bible says that we are the temples of God.

"Know ye not that ye are the temple of God, and that the Spirit of God dwelleth in you?" – 1 Corinthians 3:16

We are temples. God took the female part of man out and made Woman, Now there were two to make one: male and female to make man. Genesis 2:23 says, "bone of my bone and flesh of my flesh," and Adam acknowledges something that was made just as he was.

The fall of man

Most anyone who was raised in church can remember an image of the serpent tempting Eve with an apple because the Apple was the forbidden fruit and while it may have been a pear farmers attempt to monopolize a fruit market, that isn't at all how it happened. The fruit Eve was tempted with was not a literal fruit that you can find at a grocery store, but Eve was tempted with the fruit of righteousness because she believed it would make her as gods; notice the plural. Eve was in the form gods when she was part of man: male and female, but now she was only female. The temptation of the serpent was one of restoration.

"For God doth know that in the day ye eat thereof, then your eyes shall be opened, and ye shall be as gods, knowing good and evil." – Genesis 3:5

As long as she ate from the tree of life she was trusting God for her righteousness through his leading. As soon as she ate from the tree of the knowledge of good and evil she depended on herself to be the judge of what was right and wrong. She blasphemed, or disrespected, God (Holy Spirit) by attempting to have her own righteousness and this is the one thing that cannot be forgiven (Matthew 12:31). Then Adam came along and ate of this fruit also. They realized they were naked (without God) and covered themselves in fig leaves (Law) and hid.

God asked Adam where he was and when Adam said he was naked God asked him who told him that. Not because God didn't know but because the serpent was someone Adam had authority over. Adam basically said that it was Gods fault for his descent because the woman He gave Adam gave it to him and he ate it. He passed the buck. I don't know what would have happened but if Adam would have taken responsibility and asked for forgiveness but this might have end differently

This is where God covered Adam and Eve with skins.

"Unto Adam also and to his wife did the Lord God make coats of skins, and clothed them." – Genesis 3:21

Some translations say something like clothed them with animal skins. This narrative can then be used to atone Adam and Eves sin because sin is atoned with the blood of a sacrifice. That is a false narrative because God scarified a lamb to atone sin before the foundation of the world (Revelation 13:8). The story of sacrificing animals fits the story of the way God does things but if we look at "coats of skin" in the Strongs concordance of theKJV. We can see what the translators used to write the English narrative.

"Coats" is Strongs H3801 and is defined as kᵉthôneth, keth-o'-neth; or כֻּתֹּנֶת kuttôneth; from an unused root meaning to cover (compare H3802); a shirt:—coat, garment, robe.

"Of skin" is Strongs H578 'ôwr, ore; skin (as naked); by implication, hide, leather:—hide, leather, skin.

The word "animal" is not included in the KJV and there is nothing that indicates the coat is a hide or leather. God making a leather coat takes more imagination than man being given an earthen vessel: vehicle, to live in (This scripture explains where man got a physical body)

Genesis 3:22-24

22 And the Lord God said, Behold, the man is become as one of us, to know good and evil: and now, lest he put forth his hand, and take also of the tree of life, and eat, and live forever:

23 Therefore the Lord God sent him forth from the garden of Eden, to till the ground from whence he was taken.

24 So he drove out the man; and he placed at the east of the garden of Eden Cherubims, and a flaming sword which turned every way, to keep the way of the tree of life.

God didn't want man to live forever in a fallen state, so he set him out of the garden (the Spirit) where everything has been created and is good. God then sealed it with a flaming sword.

Now during this process the serpent who is a seraphim, angel under Lucifer's throne, is told that he cursed above all cattle and he will go on his belly and eat dust for the rest of his life.

As Genesis 3:14 tell us...

"And the Lord God said unto the serpent, Because thou hast done this, thou art cursed above all cattle, and above every beast of the field; upon thy belly shalt thou go, and dust shalt thou eat all the days of thy life."

This is where sin came into the world. We can corroborate this story in Revelation

"Wherefore, as by one man sin entered into the world, and death by sin; and so death passed upon all men, for that all have sinned:" – Romans 5:12

"And the great dragon was cast out, that old serpent, called the Devil, and Satan, which deceiveth the whole world: he was cast out into the earth, and his angels were cast out with him." – Revelation 12:9

You might be asking where I came up with this? I just read the Bible and view it as an eternal document where all verses interact with each other. I have just been led to connect the dots. The Bible says that we are priests and kings in God's Kingdom (Revelation 1:6) and then the Bible also tells us that it is God's glory to conceal things in his Word for kings to uncover, or search it out. So I am well qualified to be writing this. Let's start with Jesus in the Garden...

Jesus said He saw Satan being cast out of Heaven and He (Jesus) watched him fall like lightning. It doesn't matter many how many times I read Genesis, I can only find mention of God, Adam and Eve in the garden, but Jesus says,

"And he said unto them, I beheld Satan as lightning fell from heaven." – Luke 10:18

So where was Jesus?

The Bible also says that Jesus is the wisdom of God.

"But unto them which are called, both Jews and Greeks, Christ the power of God, and the wisdom of God." – 1 Corinthians 1:24

Wisdom, in Proverbs, is defined as "a tree of life.

She (wisdom) is a tree of life to them that lay hold upon her: and happy is every one that retained her. – Proverbs 3:18

This would make Jesus the Tree of Life. Then Jesus says in John 15:1 that "He is the one true vine" and this, in my opinion, is Jesus saying I am the tree of life. Jesus said

"Jesus saith unto him, I am the way, the truth, and the life: no man cometh unto the Father, but by me. – John 14:6

Then He compares himself to a tree/vine with branches a few verses later and for these reasons I would call Him the Tree of Life based on scripture

I am the vine, ye are the branches: He that abideth in me, and I in him, the same bringeth forth much fruit: for without me ye can do nothing. -John 15:5

What is your tree covered with

Jesus was with Adam and Eve in the Garden the same way He is with us in our "garden": work, family, church, marriage, etc. In John 16:7, it says that He (Jesus) has to leave but he is sending back a "comforter" to help us (that's the Holy Spirit). These are His fruit, in Galatians 5:22-23:

"But the fruit of the Spirit is love, joy, peace, longsuffering, gentleness, goodness, faith, meekness, temperance: against such there is no law."

These are the fruits we are to eat. This would be what Paul calls "spiritually-minded" because if we follow the Spirit we will complete the righteousness that is in the law (Galatians 8:4).

These are the fruit, or works, of the flesh:

Galatians 5:19-21

19....adultery, fornication, uncleanness, lasciviousness,

20 Idolatry, witchcraft, hatred, variance, emulations, wrath, strife, seditions, heresies,

21 Envyings, murders, drunkenness, revellings, and such like

Those who do these would be called fleshly minded. People that follow the lust of the flesh, for instance.

Here's a passage from Romans 8 providing more depth to this topic...

5 For they that are after the flesh do mind the things of the flesh (G4561); but they that are after the Spirit the things of the Spirit.

6 For to be carnally minded is death; but to be spiritually minded is life and peace.

7 Because the carnal mind is enmity against God: for it is not subject to the law of God, neither indeed can be.

8 So then they that are in the flesh cannot please God.

9 But ye are not in the flesh, but in the Spirit, if so be that the Spirit of God dwell in you. Now if any man has not the Spirit of Christ, he is none of his.

What kind of things would a carnal-minded person look at? You can find in the Old Testament similar character traits being commanded against in the 10 Commandments.

Exodus 20:3-17

3 Thou shalt have no other gods before me.

4 Thou shalt not make unto thee any graven image, or any likeness of any thing that is in heaven above, or that is in the earth beneath, or that is in the water under the earth:

5 Thou shalt not bow down thyself to them, nor serve them: for I the LORD thy God am a jealous God, visiting the iniquity of the fathers upon the children unto the third and fourth generation of them that hate me;

6 And shewing mercy unto thousands of them that love me, and keep my commandments.

7 Thou shalt not take the name of the LORD thy God in vain; for the LORD will not hold him guiltless that taketh his name in vain.

8 Remember the sabbath day, to keep it holy.

9 Six days shalt thou labour, and do all thy work:

10 But the seventh day is the sabbath of the LORD thy God: in it thou shalt not do any work, thou, nor thy son, nor thy daughter, thy manservant, nor thy maidservant, nor thy cattle, nor thy stranger that is within thy gates:

11 For in six days the LORD made heaven and earth, the sea, and all that in them is, and rested the seventh day: wherefore the LORD blessed the sabbath day, and hallowed it.

12 Honour thy father and thy mother: that thy days may be long upon the land which the LORD thy God giveth thee.

13 Thou shalt not kill.

14 Thou shalt not commit adultery.

15 Thou shalt not steal.

16 Thou shalt not bear false witness against thy neighbour.

17 Thou shalt not covet thy neighbour's house, thou shalt not covet thy neighbour's wife, nor his manservant, nor his maidservant, nor his ox, nor his ass, nor any thing that is thy neighbour's.

That's why these are known as the carnal commandments, because people are trying to control their flesh in their own strength, but really that just gives more strength to sin in their flesh.

"The sting of death is sin; and the strength of sin is the law." - 1 Corinthians15:56

That is why we are to follow the leading of the spirit because it will complete the righteousness of the law!

"That the righteousness of the law might be fulfilled in us, who walk not after the flesh, but after the Spirit." – Romans 8:4

Now we have a new High Priest...

"Who is made, not after the law of a carnal: g4559: governed by mere human nature, commandment, but after the power of an endless life." – Hebrews 7:16

A carnal-minded Christian is one who loves his neighbor as himself or follows any of the other laws of Moses. Now I am not trying to say that we forget the Law of Moses. We know that the law is good, if a man uses it lawfully.

8 But we know that the law is good, if a man use it lawfully;

9 Knowing this, that the law is not made for a righteous man, but for the lawless and disobedient, for the ungodly and for sinners, for unholy and profane, for murderers of fathers and murderers of mothers, for manslayers,

10 For whoremongers, for them that defile themselves with mankind, for menstealers, for liars, for perjured persons, and if there be any other thing that is contrary to sound doctrine – Timothy 1:8-10

"For the priesthood being changed, there is made of necessity a change also of the law." – Hebrews 7:12

Here's another passage from Hebrews 7 on this topic…

18 For there is verily a disannulling of the commandment going before for the weakness and unprofitableness thereof.

19 For the law made nothing perfect, but the bringing in of a better hope did; by the which we draw nigh unto God.

20 And inasmuch as not without an oath he was made priest:i

21 (For those priests were made without an oath; but this with an oath by him that said unto him, The Lord sware and will not repent, Thou art a priest for ever after the order of Melchisedec]

22 By so much was Jesus made a surety of a better testament.

We are ministers of this better Testament.

"Who also hath made us able ministers of the new testament; not of the letter, but of the spirit: for the letter killeth, but the spirit giveth life." – 2 Corinthians 3:6

The letter killeth? How does the letter "killeth" you might ask?

Galatians 5:4 says "Christ is become of no effect unto you, whosoever of you are justified by the law; ye are fallen from grace."

The word translated as justified is Strong's G1344 and the outline of biblical usage says it means:

To render righteous or such he ought to be

To show, exhibit, evince, one to be righteous, such as he is and wishes himself to be considered

To declare, pronounce, one to be just, righteous, or such as he ought to be

This verse is saying that if your righteousness comes from the law, or you eat from the Tree of the Knowledge or good and evil, then you fall from grace and if you were saved by grace and you fall from it are you still saved.

"For by grace are ye saved through faith; and that not of yourselves: it is the gift of God: Not of works, lest any man should boast." – Ephesians 2:8-9

This passage from Hebrews 8 should help bring a new understanding: a new level

6 But now hath he obtained a more excellent ministry, by how much also he is the mediator of a better covenant, which was established upon better promises.

7 For if that first covenant had been faultless, then should no place have been sought for the second.

8 For finding fault with them, he saith, Behold, the days come, saith the Lord, when I will make a new covenant with the house of Israel and with the house of Judah:

9 Not according to the covenant that I made with their fathers in the day when I took them by the hand to lead them out of the land of Egypt; because they continued not in my covenant, and I regarded them not, saith the Lord.

10 For this is the covenant that I will make with the house of Israel after those days, saith the Lord; I will put my laws into their mind, and write them in their hearts: and I will be to them a God, and they shall be to me a people:

11 And they shall not teach every man his neighbour, and every man his brother, saying, Know the Lord: for all shall know me, from the least to the greatest.

12 For I will be merciful to their unrighteousness, and their sins and their iniquities will I remember no more.

13 In that he saith, A new covenant, he hath made the first old. Now that which decayeth and waxeth old is ready to vanish away.

In the first covenant an Israelite could be accused of not keeping by Lucifer. Lucifer would point out where his seed, sin, was winning the battle. This was the enmity God talked about in Genesis…

And I will put enmity between thee and the woman, and between thy seed and her seed; it shall bruise thy head, and thou shalt bruise his heel. – Genesis 3:15

Jesus came to restore fellowship with God for all people, not just the Israelites, by destroying the works of the devil (1 John 3:8). The works of the devil miss the mark of righteousness, which is the definition of sin. If we can no longer sin why do we constantly fight the devil

We know that God's children do not make a practice of sinning, for God's Son holds them securely, and the evil one cannot touch them.- 1 Johni 5:18

Lucifer is not the devil.

Isaiah 14:13 states, "For thou hast said in thine heart, I will ascend into heaven, I will exalt my throne above the stars of God: I will sit also upon the mount of the congregation, in the sides of the north."

I have grown up in church hearing about how Lucifer deceived a third of the angels and tried to overthrow God. I always heard that Lucifer was a Cherub or a cute little angel that flies around the head of God playing a harp. Traditionally, I have been told he was the leader of the music ministry in heaven and his body was the culmination of different musical instruments. He flew around God's head singing praises and one day got the idea that he should be worshiped because he was above God. So, he deceived a third of the angels to follow him, and they tried to overthrow God, but were cast out of heaven. Lucifer became Satan and these angels became demons. Now they have the power to possess people and rule their lives, but for evil. These are, supposedly, the things that we fight because they are still in the realm of the spirit.

Based on what the Bible says I would call this story a little leven, I believe the devil has been defeated. These "demons" we fight are internal behaviors which internally affect the human race eternally but can be overcome with the gifts of the spirit: sanctified behaviors . While self-discipline can overcome these demons, self-discipline cannot lead to salvation. That is why we need the Holy Spirit and Salvation!

Anyway, let us get back to the deception of traditional teaching. We can break down a few verses that are traditionally understood as being a reference to Lucifer. I will try to show you what I read as opposed to what is taught.

Ezekiel 28:13-14 states: "Thou hast been in Eden the garden of God; every precious stone was thy covering, the Sardis, topaz, and the diamond, the beryl, the onyx, and the jasper, the sapphire, the emerald, and the carbuncle, and gold: the workmanship of thy tabrets and of thy pipes was prepared in thee in the day that thou wast created. Thou art the anointed cherub that covereth; and I have set thee so: thou wast upon the holy mountain of God; thou hast walked up and down in the midst of the stones of fire."

This is unanimously understood to be a reference to Lucifer. First thing I want to point out is that this says he is in the garden but he isn't a snake. Then, it provides a list of precious stones that he is covered with. The next part of the verse seems to list some instruments of some type and then it talks about him being a cherub that covereth God. I guess if I did not define those words and just tried to make a guess based on my conventional understanding of a cherub (a cute angel that plays a harp), I guess I could see a cute Lucifer flying around God playing his pipes and tabrets. I have decided not to lean on my own understanding (as instructed in the Bible) and study those words to see what is trying to be said.

In Strongs concordance the number 8596, Tabrets, means timbrel or tambourine. So I began to understand where the phrase "covered with instruments" comes from. I use the Blue Letter Bible website when I study because it lays out several different study tools in one. Along with Strongs definition, it also has Gesenius' Hebrew-Chaldee Lexicon definition and it also talks about a tambourine except in Ezekiel 28:13. Ezekiel 28:13 the word is defined as "a bezel or hollow in which a gem is set." That makes a lot of sense because the previous grouping of verses was in reference to every "precious stone was thy covering." Stones that were set with a master jewelers precision.

Pipes has everything to do with music...except it doesn't. Pipes is Strongs number 5345 and means groove, socket, hole, cavity, settings: it is a technical term relating to jeweler's work. Gesenius' Hebrew-Chaldee Lexicon says that it is compared to a pipe because it comes from the root of the word that means to bore through (like a pipe), but pipes is not suitable to the context.

From what I have studied, the verse should read, "the workmanship of your stones and their settings are set carefully in skillfully crafted sockets that were perfected on the day you were created." Verse 14 unlocks more surprises, "Thou art the anointed cherub that covereth." Reading this, and based on traditional teaching, I see a fat Lucifer circling the throne of God so I decide to see what the Bible is really saying.

Anointed in Strongs is H4473 and means in the sense of expansion; outspread (i.e. with outstretched wings):—anointed. Cherub is H3742 and means of uncertain derivation; a cherub or imaginary figure but most understand it to be a class of angels. Cherub occurs 30 times in 21 verses in the KJV and wings occurs with it and 10 times in 4 verses cherubs are referenced with an emphasis on wings.

Covereth is 5526 and means a primitive root; properly, to entwine as a screen; by implication, to fence in, cover over, (figuratively) protect:—cover, defense, defend, hedge in, join together, set, shut up. This means that the glory of God shined through Lucifer and all of his precious stones.

Precious stones signified the works of God that His glory shined through. 1 Corinthians 3:12-13 lets us know that precious stones represent works. God's glory is shown through those works. On a side note, you had better make sure God is shining through his works, which are represented by precious stones, and not your works which are represented by wood hay and stubble.

Lucifer was the head angel that covered God. This wasn't for God's protection, but was for God's glory to shine and only through Lucifer. Then Lucifer said in Psalms 8:4-6,

"What is man, that thou art mindful of him? And the son of man, that thou visitest him? For thou hast made him a little lower than the angels, and hast crowned him with glory and honour. Thou madest him to have dominion over the works of thy hands; thou hast put all things under his feet."

Lucifer then said in his heart

Isaiah 14:13, "I will ascend into heaven, I will exalt my throne above the stars of God: I will sit also upon the mount of the congregation, on the sides of the north."

This is where Lucifer sent a serpent to beguile Adam and Eve or to exalt his throne over the stars of God.

In Revelations 12:9, we can see the serpent referred to as the devil being cast out with satan: Lucifer. "And the great dragon was cast out, that old serpent, called the Devil, and Satan, which deceiveth the whole world." To find more clarity on who the serpent was, we can look at the exodus of the Israelites from Egypt.

We come to the story of when God sent fiery serpents to bite the Israelites with Numbers 21:6. "And the LORD sent fiery serpents among the people, and they bit the people; and much people of Israel died." The word "fiery" is also translated as seraphim. A seraphim is a class of angel under Lucifer's throne, when the Israelites looked upon a bronze serpent, made by Moses under God's direction. They were made well. This is a type and shadow of what happened in the garden! Lucifer exalted his throne, a seraphim serpent, over the throne of God, that consisted of Adam and Eve, by convincing them they could have their own righteousness. In believing the serpent they offended God and became servants to sin: a seraphim serpent, and they could now experience death because they were separated from God. This idea is supported by a couple of verses.

"Know ye not, that to whom ye yield yourselves servants to obey, his servants ye are to whom ye obey; whether of sin unto death, or of obedience unto righteousness?" – Romans 6:16

"Wherefore, as by one man sin entered into the world, and death by sin; and so death passed upon all men, for that all have sinned." – Romans 5:12

Adam and Eve brought sin into the world and we can see where this happened in the rest of verse 9 in Revelations 12.

"And the great dragon was cast out, that old serpent, called the Devil, and Satan, which deceiveth the whole world: he was cast out into the earth, and his angels were cast out with him." – Revelations 12:9

We can see that "he was cast out into the earth, and his angels were cast out with him," comes after a colon. That means it just adds more context or gives more of an explanation to what was previously said. "He was cast into the earth," comes after the colon that comes after Satan and is an explanation about Satan. We can see Jesus confirm this in Luke 10:18, when he says he saw Satan fall like lightning.

At the end of the word "earth" is a comma. A comma indicates a pause, but can also be used to separate items in a list. Since we already talked about Satan, the only other subject to talk about after the comma is the serpent, the devil. A comma would not be the avenue of entrance for a new subject like angels.

Revelations 12:9 says, "and his angels," and angels are the ones that attend God's throne. Earlier in chapter 12, verse 4, it talks about the dragon "drawing a third of the stars of God with him." I believe this is the verse some confuse with a third of the angels because of a wrong understanding: a little leven some might say.

Jesus is the morning star (Revelations 22:16) referring to stature while Lucifer is referred to as a morning star (Isaiah 14:12) which made more of a reference to his brightness. One of the words is translated from Greek and the other translated from Hebrew and are not the same words or used in the same context.

Remember, I said a colon adds more understanding to what was previously said and since the word angels is after a colon, it would not be introducing a new subject. It would be expounding on something that was previously introduced.

For those reasons, I believe that angels is a reference to "that old serpent, called the devil." If we reference angels in Revelations 12:9, in the Strongs we can see it is Strongs number G32 and could mean a variety of things: a messenger, envoy, one who is sent, an angel, a messenger from God. It was translated as angel 179 times and messenger 7. I find it conclusive that the same word referencing what we have discovered is the devil was used by Paul in 2 Corinthians 12:7 when referencing the thorn in his flesh: a messenger sent by Satan: the great dragon.

Paul asked God to remove this thorn three times and God's response to all three requests was the same, "My grace is sufficient for thee." According to Romans 5:20, where do we see God's grace? A religious response would be, when we are obedient and trust in Him or when we pray without ceasing. The Bible tells us that Grace abounds when sin abounds. So, if God's answer to Paul was grace, then Paul's question must have been about sin. So, what I am really trying to say is the thorn in Paul's flesh is the devil, or sin, the sin in every man and woman's flesh.

God speaks to this when He tells the serpent in the garden that the seed of the serpent will be bruised by the seed of the woman: the serpent's head being the power of sin and the woman's seed being Jesus.

"And I will put enmity between thee and the woman, and between thy seed and her seed; it shall bruise thy head, and thou shalt bruise his heel." – Genesis 3:15

The reason It had to be the seed of woman and not the seed of man is because the seed of man is cursed with sin and this is the reason why all are born into sin.

"Wherefore, as by one man sin entered into the world, and death by sin; and so death passed upon all men, for that all have sinned." – Romans 5:12

This is what happened when Lucifer (Satan): that great dragon, and that old serpent the devil were passed into the world.

"...cursed is the ground for thy sake; in sorrow shalt thou eat of it all the days of thy life;" – Genesis 3:17

The ground is now cursed and everything has been created from the ground and every seed produces its own kind.

"And God said, Let the earth bring forth grass, the herb yielding seed, and the fruit tree yielding fruit after his kind, whose seed is in itself, upon the earth: and it was so." – Genesis 1:11

And a person could say, "Yeah, that's plants," but...

"And he shall be like a tree planted by the rivers of water, that bringeth forth his fruit in his season; his leaf also shall not wither; and whatsoever he doeth shall prosper." – Psalms 1:3

The Bible covers this. This is the reason Jesus was born without sin: he was from the seed of woman. If He had been from the seed of man instead, then sin would have been getting what it deserved through Jesus' crucifixion. Instead, Jesus got what he didn't deserve and paid the price for sins actions in the flesh. It's the original defense of Double Jeopardy. You can't be charged or accused for sin in the flesh because Jesus already has been accused and convicted and served the punishment for whatever you have done past, present and future. The wages: payment of work, for sin in the flesh will always lead to natural death

I can hear those critics out there saying, "Jesus was all man and that's why he can relate to our struggles." I agree that He was a man, but he wasn't from the seed of Adam and could not have related to our struggles on a daily basis. He was tempted on all accounts as we are, to deny God's way of doing things and pursue the devils way(i.e. sin's way of doing things). These are carnal: through the flesh. We can see Jesus' struggle and victory when reading about his temptation in the dessert experience.

I believe Jesus being led to the desert is an allegory for the human race: made from dry and parched earth without water (living water), and then Jesus was tempted by the devil the same way man is tempted by sin in our dry parched bodies without water (living water). While temptation can come through several different avenues in our flesh, it will lead to the same root; it's never going to happen so you better do it yourself.

"But every man is tempted, when he is drawn away of his own lust, and enticed." – James 1:14

We get caught up in the fruit of temptation and forget about the root of temptation. We all believe, when we are tempted, that we can meet our needs faster than God. This is what the temptation was about. The devil could meet Jesus' need faster than God, but Jesus' answer was always the same, "It is written." I never once hear Jesus say, "it feels like." The reason Jesus had to go in the desert, which is an allegorical event that happened, is because He is not from the seed of Adam and did not have a man of sin in his temple. Man of sin being the devil and the temple being His body.

Temple of God

"Let no man deceive you by any means: for that day shall not come, except there come a falling away first, and that man of sin be revealed, the son of perdition; Who opposeth and exalteth himself above all that is called God, or that is worshiped; so that he as God sitteth in the temple of God, shewing himself that he is God." – 2 Thessalonians 2:3-4

Paul calls this man of sin a thorn. We traced this thorn back to the devil: that old serpent. He was cast out with Lucifer when Lucifer tried to exalt his throne above God's. He was successful and had dominion on earth until Jesus came and took back the keys to the kingdom. Sin is still here though, but no longer has dominion, and we fight its temptations daily. Like in the movie, The Matrix, where the Matrix is everywhere, sin is everywhere. Sin came into the world and everything in the world is made from the world. Our flesh, with its lust and desires is best categorized as the devil, but Christians have been reborn in the image of God with new desires called "the fruit of the spirit"; it's a certain set of skills. This is why the spirit battles the flesh. They both have their own agendas to bring righteousness and this understanding is the simplicity of the Gospel.

I can hear some saying the Word of God created everything and I will agree that it did. Hebrews 11:3 tells us, "Through faith we understand that the worlds were framed by the word of God, so that things which are seen were not made of things which do appear." Framed is Strongs number 2675 and means:

1. To render, i.e. to fit, sound, complete

2. To mend (what has been broken or rent), to repair 1. To complete 2. To fit out, equip, put in order, arrange, adjust

3. To fit or frame for one's self, prepare 3. Ethically: to strengthen, perfect, complete, make one what he ought to be

God's words were the blueprint of creation, but he created, or made them, all from the ground.

Genesis 1

7 And the Lord God formed man of the dust of the ground, and breathed into his nostrils the breath of life; and man became a living soul.

9 And out of the ground made the Lord God to grow every tree that is pleasant to the sight, and good for food;

19 And out of the ground the Lord God formed every beast of the field, and every fowl of the air; and brought them unto Adam to see what he would call them: and whatsoever Adam called every living creature that was the name thereof.

This can be confusing because it isn't what we have been taught, but it is what the Bible says. The rest of Hebrews 11:3 gives an explanation, "things which are seen were not made of things which do appear." God could not have created the world and everything in it if He hadn't first spoken it into existence.. I highlight this to show that everything in the world is made from the world.

Adam and Eve tried to have their own righteousness by serving sin, the serpent, and in doing so brought him, sin, into the world. The serpent became know as the devil when God cursed the serpent and cast him into the world.

"And the Lord God said unto the serpent, Because thou hast done this, thou art cursed above all cattle, and above every beast of the field; upon thy belly shalt thou go, and dust shalt thou eat all the days of thy life." -Genesis 3:14

"Wherefore, as by one man sin entered into the world, and death by sin; and so death passed upon all men, for that all have sinned:" – Romans 5:12

The world we live in is a Matrix of corruption called sin, and it steals our power through deception. It tells us that the works of our flesh: adultery, fornication, uncleanness, lasciviousness, idolatry, witchcraft, hatred, variance, emulations, wrath, strife, seditions, heresies, envyings, murders, drunkenness, revellings and such like (Galatians 5:19-21), are going to meet our needs when only the fruit of the Spirit: love, joy, peace, longsuffering, gentleness, goodness, faith, meekness, temperance (Galatians 5:22-23), are the only things that will meet our needs

This is the battle of spirit and the flesh (Galatians 5:17). All I am trying to get you to do is to stop shadow boxing, or fighting an opponent that isn't there and get you to discipline your body and bring it into subjection because that's what Jesus has empowered you to do.

"I therefore run, not as uncertainly; so fight I, not as one that beateth the air: But I discipline my body and bring it into subjection, lest, when I have preached to others, I myself should become disqualified." – 1 Corinthians 9:26 – 27

The term "bring It into subjection" is Strongs G1396 and means: 1. To lead away into slavery, claim as one's slave 2. To make a slave and to treat as a slave i.e. with severity, subject to stern and rigid discipline

Carnal is the opposite of spiritual

"For to be carnally minded is death; but to be spiritually minded is life and peace." -Romans 8:6

"Let us therefore, as many as be perfect, be thus minded: and if in anything ye be otherwise minded, God shall reveal even this unto you." – Philippians 3:15

So the old way of doing things; keeping the law by offering sacrifices, making sick, or unclean people leave your camp because they did not fit the requirements of the law, is now over. Husbands who are bound to the law for righteousness no longer have to make their wives leave the house when they are menstruating because of their unclean status. The requirements of the law that controlled every aspect of life even up to cleaning yourself after intercourse have all been fulfilled through the sacrifice of Jesus. Because Jesus came to fulfill the law.

"Think not that I am come to destroy the law, or the prophets: I am not come to destroy, but to fulfill." – Matthew 5:17

This is the one law that he fulfilled.

"For the life of the flesh is in the blood: and I have given it to you upon the altar to make an atonement for your souls: for it is the blood that maketh an atonement for the soul." – Leviticus 17:11

What made Jesus' sacrifice so much more significant? Why couldn't we just continue the practice of sacrificing sheep and goats for our sins. If we go back to the story of the creation, we can see that all the beasts were made from the earth and therefore had sin or a blemish. Jesus was a spotless sacrifice because he was not from the seed of Adam. We learned in Genesis that every seed produces after its kind.

"And God said, Let the earth bring forth grass, the herb yielding seed, and the fruit tree yielding fruit after his kind, whose seed is in itself, upon the earth: and it was so." – Genesis 1:11

This is why all men are born into sin.

"Wherefore, as by one man sin entered into the world, and death by sin; and so death passed upon all men, for that all have sinned." – Romans 5:12

Mary's baby daddy wasn't Joseph. It was God and since every seed bears after its own kind, Jesus was born without sin. This is why He is called the second Adam because he was the second man created without sin. God prophesied this in the garden.

"And I will put enmity between thee and the woman, and between thy seed and her seed; it shall bruise thy head, and thou shalt bruise his heel." – Genesis 3:15

Woman does not plant a seed, man does, so every seed that Adam plants will pass sin in the next generation. Eve does not have the same responsibility so when Mary was impregnated by the Holy Spirit there wasn't a way for sin to be passed.

"And the angel answered and said unto her, The Holy Ghost shall come upon thee, and the power of the Highest shall overshadow thee: therefore also that holy thing which shall be born of thee shall be called the Son of God." – Luke 1:35

Son of God, not son of Adam. Jesus does refer to himself as the son of man, but that isn't a gender specific term. It is a reference to mankind and we learned in Genesis that man was created both male and female.

While Jesus could relate with being hungry or thirsty, I can say he never had the thought of stealing to fulfill those desires. In contrast…

"But every man is tempted, when he is drawn away of his own lust, and enticed." – James 1:14

While Jesus did have lust, or strong desires, he was never enticed to fulfill them in His own power because he wasn't a seed of Adam and did not have a man of sin living in his temple. This is the work man is enticed with to fulfill his own desires.

Galatians 5

19 Now the works of the flesh are manifest, which are these; Adultery, fornication, uncleanness, lasciviousness,

20 Idolatry, witchcraft, hatred, variance, emulations, wrath, strife, seditions, heresies,

21 Envyings, murders, drunkenness, revellings, and such like: of the which I tell you before, as I have also told you in time past, that they which do such things shall not inherit the kingdom of God.

This is why….

"…that man of sin be revealed, the son of perdition; who opposeth and exalteth himself above all that is called God, or that is worshiped; so that he as God sitteth in the temple of God, shewing himself that he is God." – 2 Thessalonians 2

Jesus didn't have a man of sin in His temple (1 Cor 6:19) to say that the flesh way is the best way.

Fast forward to the river with John the Baptist and we see Jesus being baptized and the Holy Spirit falling on Him.

"And the Holy Ghost descended in a bodily shape like a dove upon him, and a voice came from heaven, which said, Thou art my beloved Son; in thee I am well pleased." – Luke 3:22

Jesus is now…"full of love, joy, peace, longsuffering, gentleness, goodness, faith, meekness, temperance: against such there is no law." Galatians 5:22-23

This is why Jesus said I only do what my father tells me.

"For I have not spoken of myself; but the Father which sent me, he gave me a commandment, what I should say, and what I should speak." – John 12:49

He didn't have a man of sin in His flesh to tell him differently because he wasn't a seed of Adam. Man has his flesh yelling at him to do one thing while the Spirit of God is trying to lead him in a different direction. This is the battle of the Spirit and the flesh.

"For the flesh lusteth against the Spirit, and the Spirit against the flesh: and these are contrary one to the other: so that ye cannot do the things that ye would." – Galatians 5:17

The devil is the flesh

The book of John has some great truths and a verse resonated with me in a way it had not in the past. It gives us some insight into who the devil is.

"Ye are of your father the devil, and the lusts of your father ye will do. He was a murderer from the beginning, and abode not in the truth, because there is no truth in him. When he speaketh a lie, he speaketh of his own: for he is a liar, and the father of it." – John 8:44

Jesus is talking to a group of pious religious leaders and drops some truth bombs about the One His Father who sent Him. He challenged their position as descendants of Abraham by saying that they did not do the works of their father Abraham. The only work we see Abraham perform is he was able to believe: a verb, no matter what his body told him.

Romans 4

19 And being not weak in faith, he considered not his own body now dead, when he was about an hundred years old, neither yet the deadness of Sarah's womb:

20 He staggered not at the promise of God through unbelief; but was strong in faith, giving glory to God;

21 And being fully persuaded that, what he had promised, he was able also to perform.

22 And therefore it was imputed to him for righteousness.

If your father is the devil and the lust of the father you will do is supposed to define you, I guess we should find out what those lust are so we can stay away from the devil. Lust is Stongs G1939 and means…desire, craving, longing, desire for what is forbidden, lust. This same word is used in Romans…

"Let not sin therefore reign in your mortal body, that ye should obey it in the lusts G1939 thereof in AZ." – Romans 6:16

"What would the lust, or the works, of the body be…adultery, fornication, uncleanness, lasciviousness, idolatry, witchcraft, hatred, variance, emulations, wrath, strife, seditions, heresies, envyings, murders, drunkenness, revellings, and such like." – Galatians 19-21

If these lusts are of your father and the father is the devil then deductively speaking the flesh is the devil. The devil is sin and when we try to use the law for righteousness we are giving power to the devil, or sin.

"The sting of death is sin, and the strength of sin is the law." – 1 Corinthians 15:56

That is why we use the gifts of the Spirit: they are the power of God. Spirit lead righteous behavior is where it's at because then nothing is owed to us. Part of the appeal of the Law is that we feel as if we can use it as a bargaining chip with God because he owes us something. If God owed us something it wouldn't be of grace: His ability, because it would be owed to us because of our ability

"Now to him that worketh is the reward not reckoned of grace, but of debt." – Romans 4:4

This is why we cannot take credit for the things we are called to do.

"Faithful is he that calleth you, who also will do it." – 1 Thessalonians 5:24

The sin in our flesh makes it difficult to do those things, sometimes, and this is why the Spirit battles the flesh.

"For the flesh lusteth against the Spirit, and the Spirit against the flesh: and these are contrary one to the other: so that ye cannot do the things that ye would." – Galatians 5:17

Romans 7 touches on this concept.

"For the good that I would I do not: but the evil which I would not, that I do. Now if I do that I would not, it is no more I that do it, but sin that dwelleth in me." – Romans 7:19-20

The Bible refers to this as the inner and outer man.

"Therefore we do not lose heart. Though outwardly we are wasting away, yet inwardly we are being renewed day by day." – 2 Corinthians 4:16

Paul takes this a little farther in 1 Corinthians by saying:

"The first man is of the earth, earthy; the second man is the Lord from heaven."

The first man is a reference to Adam, who let sin into the world, and he is earthly, because he was made from the dust of the earth. Sin was cast into the world and would give sin dominion over everything because everything is made from the dust of the word. Adam was given a coat of skin, an earthly vehicle or earthen vessel, to navigate the world. Sin has dominion over everything that is in the world and made from the world. This is the outer man.

The Inner man is a reference to the Lord, who is Jesus, and is who we truly are. The Spirit (of the Lord) is sealed inside (Ephesians 1:13) once we believe and confess that Jesus is Lord. We are given by that Spirit all things that pertain to life and godliness and are blessed with every spiritual blessing (2 Peter 1:3). We are no longer from this word and have been given dominion over all things and given a coat/robe of righteousness (Isaiah 61:10). This is the inner man.

This is our internal, eternal battle.

Sin is the "thorn" Paul refers to being in the flesh. This thorn is also every man's/woman's battle and we can see how this happened if we read the Bible and not just read into it what we think we have been taught. Jesus said he was there when He saw Satan fall like lightning because Jesus is the tree of Life and was in the garden. Where in the Bible though does it talk about this event?

"And the great dragon was cast out, that old serpent, called the Devil, and Satan, which deceiveth the whole world: he was cast out into the earth, and his angels were cast out with him. And I heard a loud voice saying in heaven, Now is come salvation, and strength, and the kingdom of our God, and the power of his Christ: for the accuser of our brethren is cast down, which accused them before our God day and night." – Revelations 12:9-10

I want to again point out there are two players in this verse, but growing up, I always believed them to be the same player. There is Satan who is introduced as a dragon and an old serpent before being named the devil, The verse then says he, referring to Satan, was cast into earth and his angels with him. This is where I believe people get the misconception that God lost a third of the angels to Satan. No where in the Bible is there a story that God lost a third of the angels. In the beginning of chapter 12, in the 4th verse, the verse talks about the dragon, who is defined as the devil, drawing a third of stars of heaven and casting them to the earth. There are a bunch of things wrong with the theory of stars being a reference to angels that fell and I want to show you what I have discovered and understand that helped me form this opinion.

For there to be a third of anything, there has to be a finite number to begin with. A person cannot have a third of an infinite amount and that is how many angels the Bible says there are.

"22 But ye are come unto mount Sion, and unto the city of the living God, the heavenly Jerusalem, and to an innumerable company of angels." – Hebrews 12

"And I beheld, and I heard the voice of many angels round about the throne and the beasts and the elders: and the number of them was ten thousand times ten thousand, and thousands of thousands." – Revelations 5:11

The last part of verse of Revelations 5:11 appears to give a finite number. G3461 is the word that was translated and it was translated as several other finite numbers but it was also translated as infinite. Since I don't want to place limits on a limitless God I am going to believe that ⅓ isn't a reference to angles.

Second, I guess people just assume stars of heaven is a reference to angels, but I don't know why. There is a verse that says, "Lucifer is the morning star," so I can see why people would rationalize stars of heaven being a reference to angels, but then there is a verse that says Jesus is the morning star also.

"How you have fallen from heaven, morning star, son of the dawn! You have been cast down to the earth, you who once laid low the nations." – Isaiah 14:12

The King James Version puts It this way…

"How art thou fallen from heaven, O Lucifer, son of the morning! How art thou cut down to the ground, which didst weaken the nations!"

The verse refers to him as "the morning star, or son of the dawn." I deduce that some automatically assume that it is referring to the sun. I am sure there have been sermons preached, evangelically, to drive this point home about Lucifer being a star. This would make the reference to stars of God a reference angles because Lucifer is a fallen angle. These things, in my opinion, have not been researched because there is a verse that says Jesus is the morning star.

"Jesus has sent mine angel to testify unto you these things in the churches. I am the root and the offspring of David, and the bright and morning star." – Revelation 22:16

I am sure this is where the theories about Jesus and Satan being brothers, and how religion is just a fight from them and they are ultimately on the same side come from. Morning star in Isaiah 14:12 is Strongs H7837 and Strongs defines it as:

Dawn (literal, figurative or adverbial):—day(-spring), early, light, morning, whence riseth.

This, in my opinion, is more of a reference to him and not his position since the name Lucifer means light bearer. One of the references is in Greek while the other is in Hebrew.

Revelation 22:16 says "the bright and morning star," and bright is a reference to radiance because we are to be in the Light as He is in the light(1 John 1:7). But morning was translated from G3720 and means:

Based on Strongs: from G3722; relating to the dawn, i.e. matutinal (as an epithet of Venus, especially brilliant in the early day):—morning.

Star is Strongs g792 and means star (as strown over the sky), literally or figuratively:—star. The term morning star from the two verses have nothing to do with one another. One is the translation of one term while the other is the translation of 2 different terms. To say that stars of God is a reference to angles that fell would not be consistent with what the Bible teaches. It sounds like a salesperson's best attempt to get you to buy what he is selling!

Since Jesus is the morning star and we, mankind, are Joint heirs with Christ.

"And if children, then heirs; heirs of God, and joint-heirs with Christ; if so be that we suffer with him, that we may be also glorified together." – Romans 8:17

If Jesus is a star that would make mankind stars as well and God speaks to this truth.

"And I will make thy seed to multiply as the stars of heaven, and will give unto thy seed all these countries; and in thy seed shall all the nations of the earth be blessed;" - Genesis 26:4

God is referring to believers who will also believe, like their father Abraham, and have it counted to them as righteousness who will be as the stars in heaven. Now apply that truth to Revelations 12:4, when the dragon, who is sin or the devil, drew a third of the stars of God, or Abraham's descendants, to the earth. There is a past, present and future time to come and the third that was drawn to earth was a reference to man because we are in the present time.

"For I reckon that the sufferings of this present time are not worthy to be compared with the glory which shall be revealed in us." – Romans 8:18

Why are we suffering at this present time?

"…Woe to the inhabitants of the earth and of the sea! For the devil to come down unto you, having great wrath…" – Revelations 12:12

This is where sin was cast into the world.

"Wherefore, as by one man sin entered into the world, and death by sin; and so death passed upon all men, for that all have sinned:" – Romans 12:12

Now this only works if everything in the world was made from the world after it was spoken into existence by God. It had to exist in the Spirit first before it can be made in the natural world.

"Through faith we understand that the worlds were framed by the word of God, so that things which are seen were not made of things which do appear." – Hebrews 11:3

We can see this format replicated in the Bible.

"We having the same spirit of faith, according as it is written, I believed, and therefore have I spoken; we also believe, and therefore speak;" – 2 Corinthians 4:13

King David actually said it first.

"I believed, therefore have I spoken…" – Psalms 116:10

It has to be done in Heaven so that it can be done on earth. Once God saw that everything was good, He formed all of creation from the earth.

Genesis 2

7And the Lord God formed man of the dust of the ground, and breathed into his nostrils the breath of life; and man became a living soul.

9And out of the ground made the Lord God to grow every tree that is pleasant to the sight, and good for food;......

19And out of the ground the Lord God formed every beast of the field...

We can see God speaking these things into existence in the first chapter of Genesis but they were not created untill the second chapter.

Then sin was cast into the world when Adam and Eve offended God by eating the fruit of their own righteousness. Now everything from the world, including the seed of Adam, is born into sin.

"Therefore, just as through one man sin entered into the world, and death through sin, and so death spread to all men, because all sinned." – Romans 5:12

Cain't accept your sacrifice

"Ye are of your father the devil, and the lusts of your father ye will do. He was a murderer from the beginning, and abode not in the truth, because there is no truth in him. When he speaketh a lie, he speaketh of his own: for he is a liar, and the father of it." – John 8:44

"If thou doest well, shalt thou not be accepted? And if thou doest not well, sin lieth at the door. And unto thee shall be his desire, and thou shalt rule over him. And Cain talked with Abel, his brother: and it came to pass, when they were in the field, that Cain rose up against Abel, his brother, and slew him." – Genesis 4:7-8

If we read the Bible, we see that Abel brought sacrifices of the first fruit of his flock of sheep to God and God found this acceptable while Cain brought the sacrifice of the first fruit of the ground. God didn't find this acceptable because God had cursed the ground (Genesis 3:17). This is how we know God has a sense of humor. He looks at them and says, "I am Able to accept this offering, referring to Ables, but I cain't accept this one" referring to Cains. Cain's response to his disappointment was a work of the flesh: murder. A good question to ask oneself would be, if Cain committed murder, where was God's warning about sin? We can find Gods direction in scripture

If thou doest well, shalt thou not be accepted? And if thou doest not well, sin lieth at the door. And unto thee shall be his desire, and thou shalt rule over him. -Genesis 4:7

Cain was tempted with the lust of his flesh (James 1:14). And this is why he was tempted:

"...that man of sin be revealed, the son of perdition; who opposeth and exalteth himself above all that is called God, or that is worshiped; so that he as God sitteth in the temple of God, shewing himself that he is God." – 2 Thessalonians 2:3-4

We know that all men are tempted by their flesh (James 1:14) because it has sin living inside of the flesh saying that righteousness comes when you...

19 Adultery, fornication, uncleanness, lasciviousness,

20 Idolatry, witchcraft, hatred, variance, emulations, wrath, strife, seditions, heresies,

21 Envyings, murders, drunkenness, revellings, and such like – Galatians. 5

Since Cain was born after the fall of mankind he had a man of sin that sits in the temple of God, his body and tries to entice him to enjoy life is through adultery, fornication, uncleanness, lasciviousness, idolatry, witchcraft, hatred, variance, emulations, wrath, strife, seditions, heresies, envyings, murders, drunkenness, revellings, and such like. These are the lusts of the flesh and these things feel good to the flesh because they exploit its weakness.

This is how the law gives the flesh more power. It says, "Look what I did! Look at how righteous I can be in my own strength!" Following the law puffs up the flesh, the fruit of the Spirit: love, joy, peace, longsuffering, gentleness, goodness, faith, meekness, temperance (Galatians 5:22-23), pacifies. These are gifts and cannot be done in your own power unless you follow the law, but that righteousness is filthy rags to God (Isaiah 64:6). If you can earn your reward by keeping the law then your reward isn't: it Is compensation.

"Now to him that worketh is the reward not reckoned of grace, but of debt. But to him that worketh not, but believeth on him that justifieth the ungodly, his faith is counted for righteousness." – Romans 4:4-5

Christians have traded the law of Moses for the law of faith. It seems that only those with strong faith get the blessing that adds no sorrow to it. I want to say there is no more faith available than what you already have. I have heard it called logistics, The people who seem to have more faith only understand things at a different level than those who don't seem to have faith. If your blessing was based on the amount of faith you have, then your blessing would be out of debt and not out of the abundance of righteousness. Jesus already paid all debts and you have been blessed with all spiritual blessing (Ephesians 1:3) when you accept Christ as your savior because you are sealed with the Spirit of promise (Ephesians 1:13).

You now have all things that pertain to life and godliness (2 Peter 1:3) because of your obedience to the law of faith, or that's how I feel most people in church read it. You really have all things that pertain to life and godliness through our knowledge of Christ because called us by his own glory and goodness. This has nothing to do with me because God will finish the work He called me to do (1 Thessalonians 5:24).

We get so caught up with the minor things in the Bible that we miss the major things. I believe there is the saying, "We can't see the forest because of the trees." We go to church and expect to see the church of Acts with all of the signs and wonders and demonstrations of the spirit. A lot of the time, we create what we are expecting because I have noticed that when these same people go to other churches their move of God isn't the same. Just because you don't see a person being demonstrative doesn't mean God isn't moving. I know there is a different "anointing" for every church body, but that concept is not entirely true because God doesn't hold back

His anointing for special people or groups. There is one anointing but there are different facets of that anointing and everybody operates in it differently based on their knowledge and understanding. Saying that God pours anointing on some people and not others is an example of a hole-y gospel, or a gospel full of holes, one that leaves you striving to achieve the perceived pinnacle of Christianity: faith, so that you too can operate in the spirit like that person admire

I think demonstrations of the spirit have less to do with the Spirit of God and more to do with the comfort of the flesh. Demonstrations are not the power of God. The power of God is realized through renewing the mind (Romans 12:2) to His knowledge and understanding. We stop there and have created a Christianity hole that has to be filled with our works of faith and demonstrations. If we read the rest of the verse, we find why we are to renew our minds: that ye may prove what is good, and acceptable, and perfect, will of God. The children of Israel witnessed the works of God and it didn't draw them near. It had the opposite effect and made them stay away.

"Now all the people witnessed the thundering, the lightning flashes, the sound of the trumpet, and the mountain smoking; and when the people saw it, they trembled and stood far off." – Exodus 20:18

You are what you think

The world's system is about earning and taking, while the Kingdom of God is about giving and receiving. God didn't give us power to work for provision. He gave us power to receive it. This isn't a bean bag gospel where you sit in a bean bag chair and stare at a lava lamp and look for an image of Jesus. The work you perform is best described in

"For the flesh lusteth against the Spirit, and the Spirit against the flesh: and these are contrary one to the other: so that ye cannot do the things that ye would." – Galatians 5:17

So why does the flesh lust against? The works of the flesh are...adultery, fornication, uncleanness, lasciviousness, idolatry, witchcraft, hatred, variance, emulations, wrath, strife, seditions, heresies, envyings, murders, drunkenness, revellings, and such like (Galatians 5:19-21) and the works, or fruit, of the Spirit are...joy, peace, longsuffering, gentleness, goodness, faith, meekness, temperance: against such there is no law (Galatians 5:22-23). So these things are directly opposed to each other and you can see why they fight each other. Paul tells us to be spiritually minded and not carnally minded. I find it interesting they used the word carnally.

Romans 8

6 For to be carnally minded is death; but to be spiritually minded is life and peace.

7 Because the carnal mind is enmity against God: for it is not subject to the law of God, neither indeed can be.

8 So then they that are in the flesh cannot please God.

Why the distinction between carnal and flesh? In verse 6, carnally is G4561 and means...

Strong's Definitions

Σάρξ sárx, sarx; probably from the base of G4563; flesh (as stripped of the skin), i.e. (strictly) the meat of an animal (as food), or (by extension) the body (as opposed to the soul (or spirit), or as the symbol of what is external, or as the means of kindred), or (by implication) human nature (with its frailties (physically or morally) and passions), or (specially), a human being (as such):—carnal(-ly, + -ly minded), flesh(-ly).

In verse 7, carnal is G4561 and verse 8 flesh is 4561. Why do they translate the same word in Greek as 3 different words in English? I believe Hebrew 7:16 holds a key that helps us understand the intentions of the writer and not necessarily the translator. Hebrews 7:16 says "Who is made, not after the law of a carnal commandment, but after the power of an endless life." Carnal is Strongs number G4559 and means

This is where stopped

Strong's Definitions

Σαρκικός sarkikós, sar-kee-kos'; from G4561; pertaining to flesh, i.e. (by extension) bodily, temporal, or (by implication) animal, unregenerate:— carnal, fleshly.

Carnal commandment is a reference to the law of Moses and keeping the carnal commandments is a reference to the law of Moses. Romans 8, it brings on a different understanding when carnally, or carnal, is replaced with Law of Moses

"For to be Law of Moses minded is death; but to be spiritually minded is life and peace. Because the law of Moses mind is enmity against God: for it is not subject to the law (Spirit) of God, neither indeed can be. So then they that are in the flesh (the lust of) cannot please God." – Romans 8:6-8

First and second man?

"The first man is of the earth, earthy; the second man is the Lord from heaven." – 1 Corinthians 15:47

Blah, blah, blah…what does this even mean? We are born one man, fight the devil, die one man and then receive our inheritance. Our inheritance is earned based on how well we can fight the devil and resist his temptations. This is the underlying message spoken from most pulpits. The same pulpit that says that hell cannot destroy the plans God has for you can be the same pulpit that says the devil is able to steal, kill and destroy those plans. We see all the works of the devil and his supposed dark army of demons throughout the Bible and camp there.

This takes all of the responsibility off of me and puts it onto some mystical beings I can't control. These beings have somehow found their way into my life because I have, somehow, let my guard down and made myself ignorant to the devil and his devices. Some sermons seem to be all about the devil and his powerful army of demons and then the pastor will sprinkle a little salt of Jesus onto it so it will taste better when their congregation will swallow what they are being force fed. The whole time the pastor knows they are not going to fact check him because nobody reads the Bible. People just read into the Bible what they have been taught. Nobody is going to question the pastor because he Gods chosen and a person can't question Gods chosen. We can reference the story of David letting Saul live while the caves because Saul was God's chosen man for the moment. We can quote Romans 13:1 to justify our compliance

"Everyone must submit to governing authorities. For all authority comes from God, and those in positions of authority have been placed there by God." – Romans 13:1

Compliance and acceptance, without question, seem to be the pillars that Christianity is built upon. I can go to one church and hear one thing, and then go to another church and hear something totally opposite from the pulpit. I am not talking about paradoxical scriptures or teachings and I understand that God says different things to different people/congregations. I go to one church and can hear about the judgment of God and how I need to FEAR God. He could wipe me out with the clearing of a nostril but doesn't because He looks at me and sees Jesus. Then I can go to another church or sit in another service and hear about how the work of Jesus is complete but it's up to me to fight the devil. It leaves one wondering what else Jesus hasn't done?. Both of these examples have some truth in them but are not supported under the new covenant. Has the church forgotten that God finished and completed everything from the foundations of the world?

We are told to speak things in faith to create, or manifest our miracle when really we should speaking things from faith, a belief in what we can't see yet, because God has done it all. Faith is the Avenue I receive things from because Jesus, the author and finisher of faith (Hebrews 12:2), has completed it all before I even ask. This means I don't start a work or finish a work of faith and therefore I can't take credit for the work of Jesus in my life. It's a gift. I don't take credit for birthday or Christmas gifts, so why would I take credit for faith?

"For by grace are ye saved through faith; and that not of yourselves: it is the gift of God:" – Ephesians 2:8 NLT

If I try to work, faith isn't.

"Now to him that worketh is the reward not reckoned of grace, but of debt." – Romans 4:4

Believing that I have to make sure I follow all of the commandments to keep sin out of my life and for God's grace to be poured out on me is not backed up in scripture. The Bible actually says opposite of that

"Moreover the law entered, that the offense might abound. But where sin abounded, grace did much more abound." – Romans 5:20

If you look to the Old Testament for faith. Yours isn't!

"And the law is not of faith: but, The man that doeth them shall live in them." – Galatians 3:12

Paradigm Change!

"But I fear, lest by any means, as the serpent beguiled Eve through his subtlety, so your minds should be corrupted from the simplicity that is in Christ." – 2 Corinthians 11:3

The serpent, if we look in scripture, we can see is the devil (Revelation 12:9). If the devil can steal, kill and destroy then why didn't he just steal Adams authority? He had to trick them in their minds. He didn't put thoughts in their minds, but he did make them question God's authority and they sabotaged themselves. The devil: sin, is still trying to trick us today. He does this by saying that his way, or carnal ways, are better. The Bible warns us about this:

"Let no man deceive you by any means: for that day shall not come, except there come a falling away first, and that man of sin be revealed, the son of perdition; who opposeth and exalteth himself above all that is called

God, or that is worshiped; so that he as God sitteth in the temple of God, shewing himself that he is God." – 2 Thessalonians 2:3-4

This is what this man of Sin, who is the devil, tempts us with…

Galatians 5

19 Now the works of the flesh are manifest, which are these; Adultery, fornication, uncleanness, lasciviousness,

20 Idolatry, witchcraft, hatred, variance, emulations, wrath, strife, seditions, heresies,

21 Envyings, murders, drunkenness, revellings, and such like: of the which I tell you before, as I have also told you in time past, that they which do such things shall not inherit the kingdom of God.

Through this Paul lets us know that this isn't a spiritual fight: Spirit vs Spirit. This battle we fight is against our flesh and it's lust.

"For the flesh lusteth against the Spirit, and the Spirit against the flesh: and these are contrary one to the other: so that ye cannot do the things that ye would." – Galatians 5:17

These works of the flesh are a carnal force used by the sin in our flesh to tempt us with natural desires and lust. Our flesh, the devil, will tell us that its natural ways are better and a short cut to God's blessings. The gifts of the spirit are supernatural: above natural, and what God tempts us with to fight the flesh.

"But the fruit of the Spirit is love, joy, peace, longsuffering, gentleness, goodness, faith, Meekness, temperance: against such there is no law. And they that are Christ's have crucified the flesh with the affections and lusts." – Galatians 5:22-24

"But every man is tempted, when he is drawn away of his own lust, and enticed." – James 1:14

There are no curses in the Spirit.

I read there is a man of sin who sits and exalts himself above God? Now I might start to think that this is about a supernatural fight, and it is, but not like we have been taught, and I start to put on my Holy armor to fight this man of sin. Then I read the verse before…

"That ye be not soon shaken in mind, or be troubled, neither by spirit, nor by word, nor by letter as from us, as that the day of Christ is at hand." – 2 Thessalonians 2:2

Shaken in my mind? Why is this not telling me to put on my Righteous Armor? It does say spirit but if we study the word spirit to show ourselves approved. Spirit is defined by Thayer's Greek Lexicon as meaning the vital principle by which the body is animated. This verse is telling us not to be shaken by what we think because what we think will produce actions . This is why we are to renew our minds.

"And be not conformed to this world: but be ye transformed by the renewing of your mind, that ye may prove what is that good, and acceptable, and perfect, will of God." – Romans 12:2

It's only when we renew our minds that we experience what is good, acceptable and perfect. The good news of the gospel is that it's already done. We may have to work to receive it(Hebrews 4:11), but we don't have to work to earn it. It is always in your best interest to give into the temptation of righteousness. This is foolishness to those who don't believe.

The law of Moses Is not the power of God. The Spirit is God's power…

"But if the Spirit of Him who raised Jesus from the dead dwells in you, He who raised Christ Jesus from the dead will also give life to your mortal bodies through His Spirit who dwells in you." – Romans 8:11

Now this isn't a license to sin, or break the law of Moses, Because you have been doing that without a license. This is a license to be righteous by following the leading of the Spirit even when it opposes what the law of Moses says. Key to understanding is it is the leading of The Spirit, and not the desire of the flesh

"All things are lawful unto me, but all things are not expedient: all things are lawful for me, but I will not be brought under the power of any." – 1 Corinthians 6:12

"All things are lawful for me, but all things are not expedient: all things are lawful for me, but all things edify not." – 1 Corinthians 10:23

We can see Jesus provide multiple examples of Him being led by the Spirit to break the law of Moses but he wasn't led by the sin in His flesh because Jesus wasn't from the seed of Adam and was without sin. He was filled with the Spirit and that was illustrated when the Spirit, like a dove, descended upon Him in the river when He was baptized by John. That is how He lived His life.

I have grown up thinking and believing that Jesus being without sin meant that He never broke one of the Levitical laws presented by Moses, but that was a wrong belief. Jesus went around breaking the law of Moses but was still able to perform miracles and that is why, I believe, they killed him.

Leviticus 12-15 are about being unclean, or unacceptable, before God's sight and how they dealt with those things or if you were an unclean person you were to live outside of the camp. Israelites were not to be around unclean people for their physical and spiritual health. The "clean" were not supposed to socialize with the unclean. The clean were holy, or set apart, for God. When Jesus asked the woman at the well for a drink of water her response was, but you are a Jew?

The Samaritan woman said to him, "You are a Jew and I am a Samaritan woman. How can you ask me for a drink?" (For Jews do not associate with Samaritans.[a]) – John 4:9

Footnote – (a) on verse 9 says: or do not use dishes Samaritans have used.

Why did Jews not associate with Samaritans?

"And he said unto them, Ye know how that it is an unlawful thing for a man that is a Jew to keep company, or come unto one of another nation; but God hath shewed me that I should not call any man common or unclean." – Acts 10:28

It was unlawful for Jesus, a Jew, to talk to, touch or interact on any level with anyone that was considered unclean. This is why the religious leaders hated Him so much. He performed what they considered sin: breaking the law of Moses, right in front of them but Romans tells us.

"...for whatsoever is not of faith is sin." – Romans 14:23

And we know His actions were of faith because He only did what HE heard His Father say...

"For I have not spoken of myself; but the Father which sent me, he gave me a commandment, what I should say, and what I should speak." – John 12:49

Plus we know that Jesus wasn't from the Seed of Adam and was not born into sin like the rest of mankind. Jesus was born to a woman that was under the law.

"...God sent forth his Son, made of a woman, made under the law." – Galatians 4:4

"To redeem them that were under the law, that we might receive the adoption of sons. And because ye are sons, God hath sent forth the Spirit of his Son into your hearts, crying, Abba, Father. Wherefore thou art no more a servant, but a son; and if a son, then an heir of God through Christ." – Galatians 4:5-7

This is the part I think people get confused about. The Bible says Jesus was a man but Jesus Father wasn't a man born into sin and that is why Romans 8:3 says that He was sent in the likeness of sinful flesh. His appearance came from his human Mother but His power came from God the Father. If Jesus would have been from the seed of Adam then his crucifixion would have been what the sin in his flesh deserved but Jesus is our propitiation: Romans 3:25, 1 John 2:2, 1 John 4:10. A propitiation simply means satisfaction of wrath. Jesus was punished as if he was sin, but was not from the seed of Adam. Jesus was punished for sins actions but did not have sin: a noun, in his flesh so the punishment He bore was undeserved. Since a person cannot be tried for the same thing twice, we can never be accused of any action that sin performs in our flesh because Jesus already accepted that punishment.

Here we are 2,000+ years later and we are, like a Samaritan in an inn, waiting for Jesus to return so He can pay for the more that has been spent since it has taken more than 2,000 years, or two days, for Jesus: the Samaritan, to return. You might read some of the last statement and feel like it sounded familiar and I would say you are right. The story of the Good Samaritan is a great example of loving your neighbor and that is where most people leave it.

I want to take it further. The Samaritans were enemies of those from Jerusalem, but he came upon a man from Jerusalem who had been mugged.

Mark 10

30 And Jesus answering said, A certain man went down from Jerusalem to Jericho, and fell among thieves, which stripped him of his raiment, and wounded him, and departed, leaving him half dead.

31 And by chance there came down a certain priest that way: and when he saw him, he passed by on the other side.

32 And likewise a Levite, when he was at the place, came and looked on him, and passed by on the other side.

33 But a certain Samaritan, as he journeyed, came where he was: and when he saw him, he had compassion on him,

34 And went to him, and bound up his wounds, pouring in oil and wine, and set him on his own beast, and brought him to an inn, and took care of him.

35 And on the morrow when he departed, he took out two pence, and gave them to the host, and said unto him, Take care of him; and whatsoever thou spendest more, when I come again, I will repay thee.

A priest and a Levite both passed by him. You might say, "So what? That is part of the story!" But I believe Jesus picked those two characters to illustrate something they aren't saying directly. Jesus spoke in parables so that only those who have ears to hear and eyes to see would catch it. I believe the priest and the Levite represent religion and illustrate the fact that religion or the Law of Moses: the Levitical law, will not save you. But a man who is an enemy of the man from Jerusalem came and cared for him because he was filled with compassion. This is all while the men were co considered enemies.

"…when we were enemies…" – Romans 5:10

Talking about man

"…he was moved with compassion (like the Samaritan) on them, because they fainted, and were scattered abroad, as sheep having no shepherd." – Matthew 9:36

I believe the Samaritan is a type and shadow of Jesus. A man who bound our wounds and poured wine and oil on them or anointed them. This was a reference to the Holy Spirit so that it was no longer our work, but the work of Jesus to get us to the inn to be cared for.

This may have been the first time you heard that story or the 1000th time. There are nuggets of Jesus revealed throughout the Bible. We just need to have ears and eyes to recognize them.

The church, certain denominations or non-denominations, seem to be focused on the moves of God because they believe that is when the power is at, and that's one way but not the only way. Paul's prayer isn't that more works be performed in the church. Paul prays in Ephesians that the eyes of their understanding (Ephesians 1:18) be opened so that they might know the hope of their calling.

This is
We can see Jesus doing this in scripture.

"Then opened He their (disciples) understanding, that they might understand the scriptures." – Luke 24:25

If you are having a difficult time following this then I would say you are right where other disciples of Christ were when Jesus asked them to break the law of Moses.

"Many therefore of his disciples, when they had heard this, said, This is a hard saying; who can hear it?" – John 6:60

What do you ask that was so hard for them to hear?

John

53 Then Jesus said unto them, Verily, verily, I say unto you, Except ye eat the flesh of the Son of man, and drink his blood, ye have no life in you.

54 Whoso eateth my flesh, and drinketh my blood, hath eternal life; and I will raise him up at the last day.

55 For my flesh is meat indeed, and my blood is drink indeed.

56 He that eateth my flesh, and drinketh my blood, dwelleth in me, and I in him.

57 As the living Father hath sent me, and I live by the Father: so he that eateth me, even he shall live by me.

58 This is that bread which came down from heaven: not as your fathers did eat manna, and are dead: he that eateth of this bread shall live forever.

Why was this hard to hear?

"Therefore I said unto the children of Israel, No soul of you shall eat blood, neither shall any stranger that sojourneth among you eat blood." – Leviticus 17:12

Jesus was asking the disciples to transgress the Law of Moses and was saying He was with their fathers when they delivered from Egypt. This is what we are called to do.

"This I say then, Walk in the Spirit, and ye shall not fulfill the lust of the flesh." – Galatians 5:16

Why is teaching the law of Moses bad?

"A little leaven leaveneth the whole lump." – Galatians 5:9

What is leaven? Google defines it as a "substance, typically yeast, that is used in dough to make it rise." This verse is saying that a little yeast can ruin a whole lump of dough. Taking into consideration that Jesus is the bread of life, this verse embraces the fact that a little wrong teaching can ruin good teaching that you have heard. I wrote this part around Easter time and most of us know the story about how Jesus died for our sins. Jesus was crucified and hung on a cross to pay for our sin. There seems to be an understanding that Jesus was made sin on the cross. The Bible seems to teach this same thing

"For he hath made him to be sin for us, who knew no sin; that we might be made the righteousness of God in him." – 2 Corinthians 5:21

The KJV has the words, "to be" italicized. When words are italicized in the Bible, it means that they are not in the original text, but were added by the translator to bring more understanding to the text. It doesn't in this situation and would be what I consider to be a little leaven. If you take "to be" out of the verse, it would say, "For he hath made him sin for us…" and it has a similar meaning. The words "he hath made" was translated from G4160 and could be translated as bear. This verse could read something like, "For he made him to bear sin, who knew no sin, that we might be made the righteousness of God in him." This isn't adding to the Bible, in my opinion, because there are other verses that support my interpretation.

"So Christ was once offered to bear the sins of many; and unto them that look for him shall he appear the second time without sin unto salvation." – Hebrews 9:28

24 Who his own self bare our sins in his own body on the tree, that we, being dead to sins, should live unto righteousness: by whose stripes ye were healed. - 1 Peter 2:24

This says Christ (Jesus) was offered to bear, not become, the sins of many

Then there are 3 verses that say Jesus was our propitiation. A propitiation is best defined as a satisfaction of wrath.

"Whom God hath set forth to be a propitiation through faith in his blood, to declare his righteousness for the remission of sins that are past, through the forbearance of God." – Romans 3:25

"And he is the propitiation for our sins: and not for ours only, but also for the sins of the whole world." – 1 John 2:2

"And he is the propitiation for our sins: and not for ours only, but also for the sins of the whole world." – 1 John 4:10

The words "to be" in 2 Corinthians 5:21 were added but only to voice what was believed to be implied and it doesn't change the meaning of the original text. Why am I making a major deal out of a seemingly minor detain? The first thing that comes to mind is…

"You know that He appeared in order to take away sins; and in Him there is no sin." – 1 John 3:5

The Bible would be blatantly contradicting itself if the verse really were to read Jesus was "to be" sin and not what the verse in 1 John 3:5 actually said. Jesus was supposed to be a spotless sacrifice. If he was made sin, then he wouldn't have been a spotless sacrifice.

But with the precious blood of Christ, as of a lamb without blemish and without spot.
-1 Peter 1:19

He would have deserved all of the punishment he experienced because that is what sin deserved. Was He still sin when He was resurrected? He didn't deserve the punishment for sin and bore the undeserved punishment anyway. Jesus was never made sin but was made a propitiation.

Jesus bore the punishment for sin so that man wouldn't have to be punished. God's wrath for sin was satisfied in the crucifixion of Jesus. Jesus was accused for all of the actions of sin and then paid for them with his death and suffering. He was without sin, not being from a seed of Adam, and did not deserve any of the punishment he received. By doing this paid the price for all of humanity.

The fear pastors try to create by saying a traumatic situation was the judgment of God for sins a person committed is a smoke and mirrors show. The "pastors" don't believe in the finished work of Christ and are putting a veil over the hearts of their listeners because they are preaching Moses: a yoke of blessing and cursing

"But even unto this day, when Moses is read, the vail is upon their heart." – 2 Corinthians 3:15

This is why the law is bad.

"Christ has become of no effect unto you, whosoever of you is justified by the law; ye have fallen from grace." – Galatians 5:4

Jesus said he came to complete the law.

"Think not that I am come to destroy the law, or the prophets: I am not come to destroy, but to fulfill." – Matthew 5:17

This is the law he came to fulfill.

"For the life of the flesh is in the blood: and I have given it to you upon the altar to make an atonement for your souls: for it is the blood that maketh an atonement for." – Leviticus 17:11

No person is going to be judged because of sin because Jesus already was. The thing a person will be judged on is their beliefs. The belief in Christ's gift of righteousness which looks like this: love, joy, peace, longsuffering, gentleness, goodness, faith, meekness, temperance: these are fruit of theSpirit, against such there is no law. Just make sure you work out of the gift of salvation and not the law of Moses

"That the righteousness of the law might be fulfilled in us, who walk not after the flesh, but after the Spirit." – Romans 8:4

Covered with fig leaves

Mark 11

13 And seeing a fig tree afar off having leaves, he came, if haply he might find anything thereon: and when he came to it, he found nothing but leaves; for the time of figs was not yet.

14 And Jesus answered and said unto it, No man eat fruit of thee hereafter for ever. And his disciples heard it.

15 And they come to Jerusalem: and Jesus went into the temple, and began to cast out them that sold and bought in the temple, and overthrew the tables of the moneychangers, and the seats of them that sold doves;

16 And would not suffer that any man should carry any vessel through the temple.

17 And he taught, saying unto them, Is it not written, My house shall be called of all nations the house of prayer? But ye have made it a den of thieves.

18 And the scribes and chief priests heard it, and sought how they might destroy him: for they feared him, because all the people was astonished at his doctrine.

19 And when he came, he went out of the city.

20 And in the morning, as they passed by, they saw the fig tree dried up from the roots.

21 And Peter calling to remembrance saith unto him, Master, behold, the fig tree which thou cursed is withered away.

22 And Jesus answering saith unto them, Have faith in God.

23 For verily I say unto you, That whosoever shall say unto this mountain, Be thou removed, and be thou cast into the sea; and shall not doubt in his heart, but shall believe that those things which he saith shall come to pass; he shall have whatsoever he saith.

We can have whatever we say? Man that sounds too easy and all I have to do is use faith? Faith becomes a guiding principle that all of our beliefs are built on and we get more faith by hearing and hearing the word of God so that one day we too can walk on water and be just like Jesus. To be just like Jesus is what we are striving for and that is why we are known as Christians because we want to be just like Jesus: the Christ.

This type of Gospel keeps people coming back for more faith because they obviously don't have enough because they aren't having whatever they say and bad things happen to them. While I believe there is some merit to this teaching, I do not believe Mark 11 is strictly about faith and whether or not you have it, or about making sure you have enough of it. We skim through the setup of this teaching to get to what we think the point of the story is because we are trying to hear it again and again to get more faith and so we want to stay camped there because it's a goal to work towards. We feel great about ourselves when we reach goals and can bless others. Mark 11 is about righteousness. If we look at the beginning of this story we see Jesus come upon a fig tree with no fruit. I believe that is an allegory for a man under the law.

"And he shall be like a tree planted by the rivers of water, that bringeth forth his fruit in his season; his leaf also shall not wither; and whatsoever he doeth shall prosper." – Psalms 1:3

And he looked up and said, "I see men like trees, walking." – Mark 8:24

These verses correlate manto a tree. Man being alluded to as a tree is a common theme throughout scripture.

"To appoint unto them that mourn in Zion, to give unto them beauty for ashes, the oil of joy for mourning, the garment of praise for the spirit of heaviness; that they might be called trees of righteousness, the planting of the Lord, that he might be glorified." – Isaiah 61:3

"The righteous shall flourish like the palm tree: he shall grow like a cedar in Lebanon." – Psalm 92:1

"For he shall be like a tree planted by the waters, Which spreads out its roots by the river, And will not fear when heat comes; But its leaf will be green, And will not be anxious in the year of drought, Nor will cease from yielding fruit." – Jeremiah 17:8

And there are way more if you want to search them out…

Tree covered with Fig leaves…

This reference of fig leaves takes me back to the Garden of Eden where Adam and Even had fashioned a type of clothing out of fig leaves to cover

(Genesis 3:7) the sin they had just let into the world (Romans 5:12). This would make fig leaves a reference to the law because the law covers sin.

Going back to the story of Jesus and the fig tree we can now look at it as if Jesus came upon a "man" whose Righteousness was through the law and he was trying to cover his sin. Why does it point out that there was no fruit growing on the tree? If we use the Bible as a reference we can see that fruit is a reference to the Spirit of God and all of its attributes

"But the fruit of the Spirit is love, joy, peace, forbearance, kindness, goodness, faithfulness, gentleness and self-control. Against such things there is no law." – Galatians 5:22-23

Righteousness comes by faith through that same Spirit.

"For we through the Spirit eagerly wait for the hope of righteousness by faith." – Galatians 5:5

So, this man with fig leaves has his own righteousness through the law and isn't producing the fruit of the Spirit through receiving God's righteousness. I would say that is a reference to having faith in one's own ability for righteousness versus having faith in God's ability for righteousness.

That is why Jesus says in Mark 11:22 to "have Faith in God". This is the opposite of having faith in yourself, or being covered in fig leaves. Faith in yourself is only a measure (Romans 12:3) while faith in God or, some say the faith of God, is the same as Jesus which is without measure (John 3:34).

There are some out there, if not most, that say we have to get more faith by hearing and hearing the word of God. They treat faith as a battery pack that they have to keep charged and, while there is some truth to that, to me that is a gospel full of holes, a hole-y gospel. When I read that verse I pay attention to the punctuation and see the "comma" that comes after hearing.

"So then faith cometh by hearing, and hearing by the word of God." – Romans 10:17

Bing.com defines a comma as a punctuation mark (,) indicating a pause between parts of a sentence. It is also used to separate items in a list and to mark the place of thousands in a large numeral.

Using the rules of a comma, the verse doesn't join hearing and hearing together it actually separates them. Then they add the word "by" after the second hearing. While I hear preachers read the verse like this: so then faith cometh by hearing and hearing the word of God. It actually reads: so then faith cometh by hearing (pause to introduce a new subject) and hearing (comes) by the word of God. The word of God is truth (1 John 1:5) and truth brings you into the light.

"But whoever lives by the truth comes into the light..." – John 3:21

Truth is everywhere so that we do not have an excuse for not knowing.

"For the invisible things of him from the creation of the world are clearly seen, being understood by the things that are made, even his eternal power and Godhead; so that they are without excuse:" – Romans 1:20

The problem with this concept is that people believe truth is salvation and stop there. Truth really leads to salvation if you continue in the words of Jesus and become His disciple.

"Then said Jesus to those Jews which believed in him, If ye continue in my word, then are ye my disciples indeed; and ye shall know the truth, and the truth shall make you free." – John 8:31-32

Truth makes you free from yourself and your righteousness. This is what Paul says about people who have their own righteousness from the law.

"Christ has become of no effect unto you, whosoever of you are justified by the law; ye have fallen from grace." – Galatians 5:4

If you are saved by grace (Ephesians 2:8) and fall from it, are you still saved? This is what Paul says about self-righteousness.

"As for the rumor that I continue to preach the ways of circumcision (as I did in those pre-Damascus Road days), that is absurd. Why would I still be persecuted, then? If I were preaching that old message, no one would be offended if I mentioned the Cross now and then—it would be so watered-down it wouldn't matter one way or the other. Why don't these agitators, obsessive as they are about circumcision, go all the way and castrate themselves!" – Galatians 5:11-12

This is what Jesus says about self-righteousness.

"Every tree that bringeth not forth good fruit is hewn down, and cast into the fire. Wherefore by their fruits ye shall know them. Not every one that saith unto me, Lord, Lord, shall enter into the kingdom of heaven; but he that doeth the will of my Father which is in heaven. Many will say to me on that day, Lord, Lord, have we not prophesied in thy name? and in thy name have cast out devils? And in thy name have done many wonderful works? And then will I profess unto them, I never knew you: depart from me, ye that work iniquity. Therefore whosoever heareth these sayings of mine, and doeth them, I will liken him unto a wise man, which built his house upon a rock: And the rain descended, and the floods came, and the winds blew, and beat upon that house; and it fell not: for it was founded upon a rock." – Matthew 7:19-25

If you are still concerned about the law of Moses I challenge you to do what the Bible says and live by the spirit (Galatians 5:25) because it will complete the righteousness that is in the law.

"That the righteousness of the law might be fulfilled in us, who walk not after the flesh, but after the Spirit." – Romans 8:4

"There is a battle between the Spirit of God inside of you and the sin in your flesh." – Galatians 5:17

Every man is tempted by the flesh (James 1:14) because they are led to believe the desires of the flesh are the way to God and His Righteousness (2 Thessalonians 2:3-4). Living by the flesh and the carnal commandments really just gives sin power.

"The sting of death is sin; and the strength of sin is the law." – 1 Corinthians 15:56j

"What shall we say then? Is the law sin? God forbid. Nay, I had not known sin, but by the law: for I had not known lust, except the law had said, Thou shalt not covet." – Romans 7:7

The Law is Holy. It isn't for a Righteous man and is actually for the exact opposite type of person.

"Knowing this, that the law is not made for a righteous man, but for the lawless and disobedient, for the ungodly and for sinners, for unholy and profane, for murderers of fathers and murderers of mothers, for manslayers, For whoremongers, for them that defile themselves with mankind, for men stealers, for liars, for perjured persons, and if there be any other thing that is contrary to sound doctrine." – 1 Timothy 1: 9-10

Because you are righteous, you are complete in Christ.

"And ye are complete in him, which is the head of all principality and power:" – Colossians 2:10

Because we have been given all things through the knowledge and glory and goodness of Him that called us.

"His divine power has given us everything we need for a godly life through our knowledge of him who called us by his own glory and goodness." – 2 Peter 1:3

I hear some saying, "What about putting on the armor of God?" My reply to those people is that is your problem. You don't believe you already have it on. Ephesians 6:10 says to be strong in the Lord and the power of his might. He tells us this not to become something we are not, but to become what we already are. If you look at the verb "be" in present tense, it is the same as "you are". If you change the synonymous terms within the structure of the sentence, we can see that putting on the armor of God isn't something we try to do because we already have it on.

The Christian walk isn't a gospel full of holes, a hole-y gospel, that some try to patch with works of faith. The believer understands this is a wholly gospel where we have been given all things pertaining to life and godliness and we struggle to renew our minds to this truth. The truth is that we are a Holy people set apart; set apart from cursing for blessing, set apart from poorness for richness, set apart from flesh for the Spirit, set apart from the devil for God.

2 Corinthians 6 MSG

1 Companions as we are in this work with you, we beg you, please don't squander one bit of this marvelous life God has given us.

2 God reminds us, I heard your call in the nick of time; The day you needed me, I was there to help.

3 Don't put it off; don't frustrate God's work by showing up late, throwing a question mark over everything we're doing.

4 Our work as God's servants gets validated – or not – in the details. People are watching us as we stay at our post, alertly, unswervingly . . . in hard times, tough times, bad times;

5 when we're beaten up, jailed, and mobbed; working hard, working late, working without eating;

6 with pure heart, clear head, steady hand; in gentleness, holiness, and honest love;

7 when we're telling the truth, and when God's showing his power; when we're doing our best setting things right;

8 when we're praised, and when we're blamed; slandered, and honored; true to our word, though distrusted;

9 ignored by the world, but recognized by God; terrifically alive, though rumored to be dead; beaten within an inch of our lives, but refusing to die;

10 immersed in tears, yet always filled with deep joy; living on handouts, yet enriching many; having nothing, "Having it all."

CONCLUSION

8Though he were a Son, yet learned he obedience by the things which he suffered; 9And being made perfect, he became the author of eternal salvation unto all them that obey him; 10Called of God an high priest after the order of Melchisedec. 11Of whom we have many things to say, and hard to be uttered, seeing ye are dull of hearing. 12For when for the time ye ought to be teachers, ye have need that one teach you again which be the first principles of the oracles of God; and are become such as have need of milk, and not of strong meat. 13For every one that useth milk is unskilful in the word of righteousness: for he is a babe. 14But strong meat belongeth to them that are of full age, even those who by reason of use have their senses exercised to discern both good and evil. – Hebrews 5

I have always heard the last part of this scripture in the context of eating spiritual food because that is what Jesus ate and this is how we should get our nourishment. I've read the verses before and the seemingly common understanding is not contextual. If we look in verse 8 it is referring to Jesus when the writer mentions Son, because of the capitalized S, and tells us He learned His obedience by the things by which he suffered. This is a revelation! I have always heard that we were to cast our sufferings into the sea. Jesus suffered and died so that we wouldn't have to experience those things in our lives. It was our right and authority. The mountains in our lives would have to listen and be cast into the sea but when they wouldn't there was always an unspoken understanding that I needed to have more faith.

I would get this faith by hearing and hearing the word of God and for my donation of 150 dollars I could get a tape series that teaches me all about getting more faith. I needed to get the sin out of my life to hear more clearly from God. I could stop sinning by following the Law of Moses because it is sin that breaks the commandments, That would just heap more guilt and shame on top of the burden of not being able to complete the law. I needed more faith so I would listen and listen to the to the Word but as soon as I broke the Law of Moses that faith would go away because I had let sin into my life.

This is an avenue the devil could steal, kill and destroy but I needed the faith that I had lost to keep that from happening. Christianity isn't this light and easy yoke Jesus had promised because there are so many subtle nuances you have to adhere to. You might become an outcast to the popular "Holy" Christian circles, and not Christ, if you do not adhere to the unspoken commandments. Koinoni, the Hebrew word for fellowship, is what connects us all in our quest to be holy like He is Holy. So, most, follow the fence: manmade, laws so that they can be accepted but in their quest for acceptance they end up selling their souls. Its Sadd u cee. No longer are joined by koinoni because it's con-I-need-ya to do what I do to feel accepted

Christ is called to be a High priest but not in the same fashion as those with infirmities: sin, in their flesh but after the power of an endless life

Who is made, not after the law of a carnal commandment, but after the power of an endless life. – Hebrews 7:16

If the law of Moses was good why would we need to change it and if we do change it would it just be more of the same??

If therefore perfection were by the Levitical priesthood, (for under it the people received the law,) what further need was there that another priest should rise after the order of Melchisedec, and not be called after the order of Aaron? - Hebrews 7:11

Because

And it is yet far more evident: for that after the similitude of Melchisedec there ariseth another priest, - Hebrews 7:15

This priest was first introduced in Genesis

Genesis 14

18 And Melchizedek king of Salem brought forth bread and wine: and he was the priest of the most high God.

19 And he blessed him, and said, Blessed be Abram of the most high God, possessor of heaven and earth:

20 And blessed be the most high God, which hath delivered thine enemies into thy hand. And he gave him tithes of all.

Now if we cross reference this scripture with the new testament scriptures we can see the this King of Peace is a type of Jesus

26While they were eating, Jesus took bread, and when he had given thanks, he broke it and gave it to his disciples, saying, "Take and eat; this is my body." 27Then he took a cup, and when he had given thanks, he gave it to them, saying, "Drink from it, all of you. 28This is my blood of the covenant, which is poured out for many for the forgiveness of sins. – Matthew 26:26-28

When Jesus broke bread and poured wine it wasn't just a symbolism of Himself. It was a practice of the priesthood He was from.

And Melchizedek king of Salem brought forth bread and wine: and he was the priest of the most high God – Genesis 14:18

The bible said Abraham gave tithes. The law of Moses had not been written yet but Abraham set the precedent of tithing. Tithing isn't an old covenant practice because it was first introduced By Abram. He planted a seed into the Priest of the Most High God. That seed was blessed and multiplied only after Abraham was tempted by God. We know that God doesn't tempt people (James 1:13). The word tempted is Strong's H5254 and means:

To test, try, prove, tempt, assay, put to the proof or test

(Piel)

To test, try

To attempt, assay, try

To test, try, prove, tempt

This word was translated as prove 20 other times in the KJV. This, I believe is an example of God chastising the ones He loves.

This is what God said after Abraham proved himself faithful:

Genesis 22

17 That in blessing I will bless thee, and in multiplying I will multiply thy seed as the stars of the heaven, and as the sand which is upon the sea shore; and thy seed shall possess the gate of his enemies;

18 And in thy seed shall all the nations of the earth be blessed; because thou hast obeyed my voice.

Abraham believed God more than what his circumstances told him and because of Abraham's obedience we have all been blessed. Abraham didn't fight the devil or satan, he didn't put on his spiritual armor, he didn't have a bible reading plan (of course there wasn't a Bible). All he did was believe God.

I feel like most "Christians" could relate to this scripture:

John 9

27 He answered them, I have told you already, and ye did not hear: wherefore would ye hear it again? Will ye also be his disciples?

28 Then they reviled him, and said, Thou art his disciple; but we are Moses' disciples.

29 We know that God spake unto Moses: as for this fellow, we know not from whence he is

It seems that the law of Moses is put upon a pedestal because Jesus, acting as a Rabi and talking to Jews, said the two most important commandments are to love god and to love people.

Most Christians are closet disciples of Moses

Matthew 22

36 Master, which is the great commandment in the law?

37 Jesus said unto him, Thou shalt love the Lord thy God with all thy heart, and with all thy soul, and with all thy mind.

38 This is the first and great commandment.

39 And the second is like unto it, Thou shalt love thy neighbour as thyself.

40 On these two commandments hang all the law and the prophets.

Really, Jesus, as a High Priest in the order of Melchizedek, gave one commandment and that is to love like He loves – John 15:12.

Hebrews 7

15 And it is yet far more evident: for that after the similitude of Melchisedec there ariseth another priest,

16 Who is made, not after the law of a carnal commandment, but after the power of an endless life.

Are you His disciple or a disciple of Moses? Seeing that you are dull of hearing, as scripture says, I believe you're a disciple of Jesus and you are blessed through Abraham by Melchizedek

Consider then how great this Melchizedek was. Even Abraham, the great patriarch of Israel, recognized this by giving him a tenth of what he had taken in battle. Now the law of Moses required that the priests, who are descendants of Levi, must collect a tithe from the rest of the people of Israel, who are also descendants of Abraham. But Melchizedek, who was not a descendant of Levi, collected a tenth from Abraham. And Melchizedek placed a blessing upon Abraham, the one who had already received the promises of God. And without question, the person who has the power to give a blessing is greater than the one who is blessed. – Hebrews 7:4-7 NLT

….If ye were Abraham's children, ye would do the works of Abraham. – John 8:39

Stop trying to twist Gods arm through obeying the law of Moses because it was never a covenant with non-Israelites. Truly follow Jesus and follow His commandment. This commandment is not a Levitical law but comes from a High Priest in the order of Melchizedek from the tribe of Juda. Moses new nothing about these people.

14 For it is evident that our Lord sprang out of Juda; of which tribe Moses spake nothing concerning priesthood. -Hebrews 7

18 For there is verily a disannulling of the commandment going before for the weakness and unprofitableness thereof.

19 For the law made nothing perfect, but the bringing in of a better hope did; by the which we draw nigh unto God.

20 And inasmuch as not without an oath he was made priest– Hebrews 7

The LORD hath sworn, and will not repent, Thou art a priest for ever after the order of Melchizedek. – Psalm 110:4

How did Jesus love if it wasn't as himself?

And the Holy Ghost descended in a bodily shape like a dove upon him, and a voice came from heaven, which said, Thou art my beloved Son; in thee I am pleased - Mark 3:22

These are the fruits of the Spirit

22But the fruit of the Spirit is love, joy, peace, patience, kindness, goodness, faithfulness, 23gentleness, and self-control. Against such things there is no law. – Galatians 5

This I say then, Walk in the Spirit, and ye shall not fulfil the lust of the flesh. - Galatians 5:16

Get Outlook for iOS

Printed in the United States
by Baker & Taylor Publisher Services